Growing Up "White Trash"

<u>DISCLAIMER</u>

THE NAMES OF THE PEOPLE MENTIONED IN THIS BOOK HAVE BEEN CHANGED WITH THE EXCEPTION OF MIKE & DAN KEARNS AND ANY OF THEIR IMMEDIATE FAMILY TO PROTECT THEIR IDENTITY BUT MORE IMPORTANTLY...WE JUST DIDN'T WANT TO HAVE TO PAY THEM!

THE MATERIAL IN THIS BOOK CONTAINS PROFANITY, DRUG USE, ALCOHOL ABUSE, SEXUAL SITUATIONS AND ADULT TOPICS! THIS BOOK MAY NOT BE SUITABLE FOR PERSONS UNDER 18. THERE IS A LOT OF "UNDERAGE DRINKING" IN THIS BOOK AND IN NO WAY DO WE ENCOURAGE OR SUPPORT THIS.

WE REALIZE THIS IS PROBABLY GOING TO BE ONE OF THE FUNNIEST BOOKS YOU HAVE EVER READ, BUT JUST LIKE "TEXTING" PLEASE DON'T READ THIS WHILE DRIVING! EITHER ONE COULD CAUSE AN ACCIDENT. ENJOY!

GROWING UP "WHITE TRASH"

A BOOK BY TWO BROTHERS WHO SHARE STORIES FROM THEIR CHILDHOOD, DETAILING WHAT IT WAS LIKE GROWING UP AS THE TWO YOUNGEST BROTHERS IN A FAMILY OF 6 BOYS (NO SISTERS) AND THE FUNNY ADVENTURES THEY GOT INVOLVED IN. THIS WAS THE 70'S & 80'S, THERE WERE NO CELL PHONES OR COMPUTERS! MUSIC WAS PLAYED ON RECORD PLAYERS AND LATER ON CASSETTE TAPES. MTV (MUSIC TELEVISION) FIRST AIRED ON AUGUST 1st 1981, BRINGING MUSIC VIDEOS TO T.V. CHANGING THE WAY WE LOOKED AT MUSIC FOR GOOD!

PEOPLE IN OUR NEIGHBORHOOD NEVER LOCKED THEIR DOORS AT NIGHT. KIDS WOULD GET UP IN THE MORNING, GET ON THEIR BIKES AND WOULD STAY GONE ALL DAY, ONLY RETURNING HOME IN THE EVENING TO EAT DINNER! IT WAS A DIFFERENT TIME THEN! A GREAT TIME TO BE A KID! WE NEVER REALIZED JUST HOW GOOD WE HAD IT UNTIL WE TOOK TIME TO LOOK BACK ON OUR CHILDHOOD AND SEE ALL THE FUN STUFF WE GOT TO DO. HOPEFULLY THIS BOOK BRINGS BACK MEMORIES OF YOUR CHILDHOOD AND THE HAPPY TIMES YOU HAD GROWING UP AS WELL! ENJOY!

A Very Special Thank You!

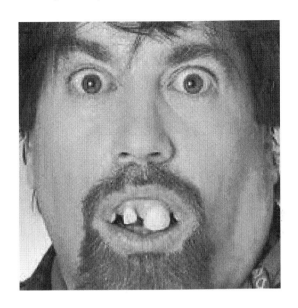

THIS BOOK WAS EDITED BY OUR COUSIN, "BILLY BOB KEARNS" FROM ARKANSAS. NOW BILLY BOB ONLY GOT AS FAR AS THE 5th GRADE BUT HE'S AS SMART AS THEY COME. WE FELT THAT WITH HIS "COMMAND OF THE ENGLISH LANGUAGE" THAT HE WOULD BE THE RIGHT MAN FOR THE JOB! PLUS, HE NEEDED THE WORK. HE JUST GOT LAID OFF AND SUE ELLEN IS PREGNANT AGAIN. SHE SHOULDN'T BE CLIMBING IN THOSE DUMPSTERS FOR CANS THIS FAR ALONG IN HER PREGNANCY! HE WOULD GIVE YOU THE SHIRT OFF HIS BACK (IF HE WORE ONE) AND A STRANGER IS JUST A FRIEND HE HASN'T MET YET!

SO, IF YOU SEE ANY TYPO'S IN THE BOOK REMEMBER THEY TALK A LITTLE DIFFERENT WHERE HE'S FROM!

ENJOY THE BOOK!

.

INTRODUCTION

GROWING UP IN A FAMILY OF (8) WHICH CONSISTED OF (6) BOYS AND NO SISTERS! THERE'S KEVIN, TIM, TERRY, PAT, MIKE AND DAN! WE GREW UP IN A VERY SMALL HOUSE, IT WAS 3 BEDROOMS AND 1 BATH. THESE ROOMS WERE THE SIZE OF SOME PEOPLE'S CLOSETS TODAY! IN FACT OUR DAD HAD TO BUILD ANOTHER ROOM OUT IN THE GARAGE JUST SO WE COULD ALL FIT! SO THAT WAS (2) TO A BEDROOM, UNTIL SOMEONE MOVED OUT, THEN THE OLDEST GOT THE ROOM IN THE GARAGE BY THEMSELVES! I DON'T THINK OUR MOM AND DAD LIKED THAT ROOM MUCH THOUGH BECAUSE IT SEEMED LIKE THERE WAS ALWAYS SOME FUNNY SMELLING SMOKE COMING OUT OF THERE AND IF YOU WALKED IN THAT ROOM THE SMELL WAS OVERWHELMING! NOT REALLY A BAD SMELL BUT JUST A DIFFERENT ONE! IF YOU STAYED IN THERE TOO LONG YOU STARTED TO GET "LIGHT-HEADED" AND YOU WOULD SMILE A LOT AND GET REALLY HUNGRY!

IT HAD ITS ADVANTAGES AS WELL AS ITS DISADVANTAGES! OUR DAD WAS A MATH TEACHER WHO HAD TO WORK (2) JOBS JUST TO AFFORD TO RAISE US. HE WOULD TEACH MIDDLE SCHOOL ALL DAY, COME HOME FOR A COUPLE HOURS, EAT DINNER AND THEN HE WOULD BE OFF TO TEACH "NIGHT" SCHOOL FOR KIDS WHO JUST COULDN'T

HANDLE "DAY" SCHOOL. OUR MOM WAS A "STAY AT HOME MOM" OR BACK THEN IT WAS REFERED TO AS A "HOUSEWIFE." WE HAD THE TWO BEST PARENTS IN THE WORLD! EVEN THOUGH WE WERE POOR OR AT LEAST LOWER MIDDLE CLASS, WE NEVER KNEW IT! I GUESS ALL OUR FRIENDS WERE LIKE US, EXCEPT NOBODY HAD (5) BROTHERS LIKE WE DID! WE THOUGHT EVERYBODY DRANK BLUE MILK. (POWDERED MILK- A MIX YOU ADD WATER TO) GROSS! AT MEALTIME AT OUR HOUSE YOU HAD TO PRAY WITH ONE EYE OPEN MAKING SURE THAT WHEN YOU SAID "AMEN" YOU KNEW JUST WHAT FOOD YOU WERE GRABBING FOR OR YOU WOULD BE S.O.L. (SHIT OUT OF LUCK). DAN AND I WERE THE TWO YOUNGEST BROTHERS, DAN BEING THE YOUNGEST AND THEN ME NEXT TO LAST. ONE ADVANTAGE WE HAD WAS THAT WE WERE GOOD IN SPORTS! WELL, DAN WAS GOOD AND I PLAYED JUST WELL ENOUGH TO NOT GET PICKED LAST WHEN PEOPLE WERE CHOOSING TEAMS! MY OLDER BROTHERS WERE ALWAYS THE MVP'S (MOST VALUABLE PLAYER) AT SCHOOL, MADE THE ALL-STAR TEAMS, WERE CAPTAINS OF THEIR TEAMS, ETC. THIS MADE OUR DAD VERY HAPPY AND PROUD! HE WOULD BE AT EVERY GAME; IN FACT WHEN I WAS ON THE "SWIM TEAM" IN HIGH SCHOOL (WHICH ALMOST NOBODY CAME TO WATCH) MY DAD WOULD ALWAYS BE AT MY RACES! I'M SURE HE WAS KINDA EMBARRASED BECAUSE I WAS OVERWEIGHT AND I HAD TO WEAR THE REQUIRED "SPEEDO" BATHING SUIT, BUT HE NEVER LET ME KNOW ANYTHING BUT

THAT HE WAS PROUD OF ME! A COUPLE YEARS LATER I PLAYED ON A MEN'S SOFTBALL TEAM AND I DID REALLY WELL AND HE GOT TO SEE ME PLAY, SO I WAS HAPPY ABOUT THAT!

BEING THE TWO YOUNGEST MEANT WE GOT A LOT OF "HAND-ME-DOWN" CLOTHES! WHEN WE DID GET TO GO SHOPPING FOR LIKE SHOES FOR INSTANCE, THERE WERE NO NIKES, ADDIDAS, OR CONVERSE FOR US, NOPE IT WAS WHATEVER WAS ON SALE AND TRUST ME IT WAS NOT NAME BRAND STUFF! THEY DIDN'T SELL NIKE'S @ KMART! HOWEVER, AS WE GOT OLDER AND OUR BROTHERS STARTED MOVING OUT OF THE HOUSE THINGS GOT BETTER AND WE STARTED TO GET SOME BETTER CLOTHES AND SHOES, ETC.

OUR DAD WAS A BIG BELIEVER IN "CORPROAL PUNISHMENT" AND WHEN THE SCHOOL WOULD SEND HOME THOSE PERMISSON SLIPS ASKING IF YOU WANTED YOUR SON OR DAUGHTER "SPANKED" AT SCHOOL OR NOT, OUR DAD WOULD ALWAYS SIGN IT YES, SPANK THEM! I THINK I WAS ONE OF THE ONLY KIDS THAT WAS ALLOWED TO GET SPANKED! NOT ONLY THAT BUT AFTER GETTING SPANKED AT SCHOOL (WHICH I HAD MY SHARE OF) I WOULD GET IT AT HOME TOO! OUR BROTHER KEVIN MADE THIS "PADDLE" IN SHOP CLASS AND GAVE IT TO OUR DAD; IT WAS CALLED "THE ORANGE PADDLE" AND IT LOOKED SCARY! I REMEMBER MANY TIMES "HIDING" THAT ORANGE PADDLE BEFORE MY

DAD GOT HOME! HE WOULD GO TO GET IT OUT OF THE GARAGE WHERE IT WAS KEPT AND WHEN HE COULDN'T FIND IT, HE WOULD BE LIKE "O.K. WHERE IS IT?" I WOULD SAY IN A TINY VOICE "I DON'T KNOW?" THEN HE WOULD RAISE HIS VOICE AND SAY, "GODDAMMIT WHERE'S THAT PADDLE?" THEN EVERYTIME I WOULD GET SCARED AND GO GET IT FOR HIM! LUCKILY, HE USUALLY ONLY GAVE ME (1) GOOD CRACK! I WAS A GREAT "CON ARTIST" SO I WOULD PLAY UP THE CRYING AND SCREAMING, BUT IT STILL HURT LIKE HELL! ONE TIME I TRIED TO PUT A PILLOW IN MY PANTS OVER MY BUTT BEFORE I GOT SPANKED BUT WHEN I BENT OVER HE SAW IT AND MADE ME PULL IT OUT! HE EVEN HAD TO LAUGH AT THAT ONE! WHAT CAN I SAY, I TRIED! I GUESS I DESERVED EVERYTHING I GOT BUT MY INTENTIONS WERE ALWAYS GOOD! I JUST WANTED TO MAKE PEOPLE LAUGH! HOWEVER, I GUESS I TOOK THINGS TOO FAR SOMETIMES? WAS IT WORTH IT? "HELL YES!"

WHO WE WERE

MIKE: (AS TOLD BY DAN)

A VERY FUNNY GUY WHO TO THIS DAY SHOULD BE A "STAND UP" COMEDIAN! HIS IMPERSONATIONS OF PEOPLE OR JUST THE MADE UP CHARACTERS IN HIS MIND WERE PRICELESS! IN SCHOOL, PEOPLE WOULD CROWD AROUND HIM TO HEAR HIM HAVE "CAPPING CONTESTS" (2 PEOPLE GO BACK AND FORTH PUTTING EACH OTHER DOWN, SAYING YOUR MOM'S SO FAT JOKES,ETC.) WITH OTHER KIDS. HE NEVER LOST! HE ALSO HAD A FASCINATION OF GETTING SOMETHING FOR NOTHING! SOME REFER TO IT AS "STEALING" BUT HE CHOSE TO CALL IT "BORROWING WITHOUT EVER PAYING IT BACK!" SOMEWHAT SUCESSFUL, BUT WOULD GET CAUGHT FROM TIME TO TIME. ALWAYS HAD A WAY OF COMING INTO SOME MONEY, BUT IT WOULD BE SPENT WITHIN MINUTES. ALWAYS GOT ALONG WITH EVERYBODY. DURING FAMILY GATHERINGS EVERYONE WOULD JUST "THROW OUT" REQUESTS FOR MIKE TO ACT SOMETHING OUT, TO BE FUNNY. HE WAS ALWAYS IN HIGH DEMAND! DEFINITELY HAD A FUTURE IN COMEDY!

DAN:

DAN WAS A TRUE ATHLETE. HE WAS BORN WITH "NATURAL ABILITY." THAT'S NOT TO SAY HE DIDN'T WORK AT IT. HE ALWAYS WORKED HARD AT ALL THE SPORTS HE PLAYED; HE JUST MADE IT LOOK EASY! ALWAYS PICKED "FIRST" IN SPORTS. LOVED AND LOOKED UP TO ALL HIS BROTHERS AS HE WAS THE YOUNGEST OF THE GROUP. AS HE GOT OLDER HE

LIKED TO DRINK AND PARTY, ALWAYS UP FOR A GOOD TIME. HE MADE FRIENDS EASILY EVERYWHERE HE WENT. LOVED TO HELP SPEND MIKE'S MONEY BUT WOULD SAVE EVERY NICKEL HE GOT!

CODY:

BY FAR THE CRAZIEST OF THE BUNCH. HE WAS NO STRANGER TO FINDING OUT HOW FAR HE COULD GO WITH SOMETHING BEFORE GETTING CAUGHT. HE HAD THE REST OF US AS HIS AUDIENCE. IF HE WAS SUCCESFUL AT STEALING CANDY, THE NEXT TIME IT WOULD BE CANDY AND BEEF JERKY. THEN JERKY AND BEER, THEN BEER AND WHISKEY, AND SO ON. HE NEVER SHYED AWAY FROM A CONFRONTATION OR A FIGHT. IF SOMEONE STARED AT HIM TOO LONG HE WOULD TALK SO MUCH CRAP UNTIL, UNFORTUNATELY THIS WOULD LEAD TO A FIGHT. CODY RARELY WON! HE WAS ALWAYS SO DAMN FUNNY AND WOULD DO ANYTHING FOR A LAUGH. MIKE CALLED HIM "THE FUNNIEST GUY HE EVER MET!"

RONALD:

A COOL DUDE. HE WAS COOL WITH DOING ANYTHING WE WANTED TO DO. I THINK THE REST OF US WERE BAD INFLUENCES ON HIM, ESPECIALLY WHEN IT CAME TO DRINKING. RONALD WAS REALLY CLOSE WITH HIS DAD. THEY WOULD LOVE TO GO FISHING AND HUNTING TOGETHER. I THINK THE HUNTING TRIPS SLOWED DOWN AFTER ONE TRIP WHERE HE AND HIS DAD WERE ON A LONG TRAIN TRESSLE AND A TRAIN CAME OUT OF NOWHERE. THEY RAN AS FAST AS THEY COULD AND NEARLY DIED! THEY ENDED UP GETTING "CLIPPED" BY THE

TRAIN. RONALD EVEN HAD TO HAVE PINS PUT IN HIS ARM. ONE GREAT GUY!

JACK:

MR. FIX IT MAN. HE WOULD LOVE TO TINKER AROUND WITH THINGS, ESPECIALLY CARS. WHEN WE WOULD GO OFF TO PARTY, SOMETIMES JACK WOULD CHOOSE TO REMAIN BACK AND MISS OUT TO FINISH A PROJECT HE WAS WORKING ON. IT WASN'T ALWAYS THAT WAY THOUGH. JACK COULD PARTY WITH THE BEST OF THEM. THE GREAT THING IS, WHEN SOMETHING WOULD GO WRONG, OR WE WOULD GET IN TROUBLE, HE WOULD ALWAYS TAKE THE BLAME. THAT'S JUST HOW HE WAS. A REAL "STAND UP" GUY!

JOE:

JOE WAS JACK'S BROTHER. WE WOULD ALWAYS TRY TO GET JOE TO DO CRAZY THINGS AND MOST THE TIME HE WOULD! HE WOULD GO STRAIGHT UP TO STRANGERS AND BE A "SMART ASS!" HE LOVED THE ATTENTION THIS BROUGHT HIM! DEFINITELY DID NOT GET ENOUGH HUGS GROWING UP! HE WAS ALWAYS FUN TO PICK ON. HE WOULD BE CONSIDERED THE "SCREW OFF" OF THE GROUP!

THE WHITE'S 50TH WEDDING ANNIVESARY

There was an old couple that moved in next door to us named "The Whites." They were a pretty nice couple, they let me mow their lawn a couple times but they were the kind of people who wanted way more than the $2.50 they were paying me (My going rate at the time) and thought I should have done a better job than the one I did for all THAT money! Needless to say, I only did their lawn a couple times! Mrs. White had a hobby…"Knitting Pretties" and these were like little hot pads, placemats, dolls made of yarn, etc. It was always funny to hear my brother Dan say, "Hi Mrs. White, How's your pretties?" No clue!

Anyway, The Whites were getting ready to celebrate their 5oth Wedding Anniversary and they were real excited! We were real excited too because we were invited (it was a BBQ being held in their Backyard) and we were happy to be able to do anything! Plus, if we got to eat and drink Soda...even better!

The Party came and they had a big turnout! The food was O.K. (we didn't like it much because it was a bunch of potato salad Crap and things Old People liked to eat more than anything) and the soda was Generic, no Coke or Pepsi but it was free! The adults were drinking Champagne and there must have been like (50) Bottles, I never saw so many! When the adults started getting a little drunk we ran next door into our backyard where we could throw Shit at the people and then "Duck and Hide." Overall it was a pretty fun day!

The next morning, I (Mike) went in the backyard to see how many cans/bottles were laying around that we could bag up and turn them in to the Recycling place for $$. As soon as I looked over the fence I couldn't believe it! There was a lot of Soda left out but more than that, there was like (30) bottles of Wine left! I ran and got my Brother (Dan) and showed him what I found. I told him we needed to get some bags and go get all that Champagne (and some sodas too!)And take them over to our friends house (Joe and Jack Johnson-Brothers) Well, their Sisters house (She lived across the street) so she would think we were the Coolest for giving her all this booze! Just like we thought, she gladly accepted it but then she called her mother (Joe and Jack's Mom) and told her about it! She then in turn called our house and told My Mom what we did and then "All Hell broke loose from there!" We had to return all the bottles to the "White's" and apologize for "Stealing" them. I remember it like it was just yesterday! They were so disappointed in us, told us how bad it was, how we basically "Ruined" their Anniversary. We felt terrible! But then the real punishment came...from our parents!

They figured out that I (Mike) was the Mastermind behind all of it and I got the brunt of the punishment! I was put on (1) month restriction (Which meant working around the house, cleaning, yard work, etc. I had tickets to the 6 Flags Park (Marriott's Great America) where I was to go to my first Music "Concert" which my Dad took away and did not let me go. No matter how hard I begged and pleaded, (and I did too) He never gave in!

Mr. White Died a couple years later and we would occasionally see Mrs. White but it was never the same! This was only the start to my career of "Borrowing" from the People!"

"BORROWING FROM LOCAL STORES"

We had a friend "Cody" who had to be one of the World's greatest "Shoplifters" in the world. This guy could steal an Ice Cube out of your drink while you were drinking it and you would never know. He was THAT good!

It was at the beginning of our "Drinking Career" (I must have been 16 and Dan was like 14, Cody was 16 as well) and of course we never had no money but still wanted to catch a "Buzz." So... we would wait until it got dark, and then we would walk down to the store (it was called Shortstop but today it's a Tower Mart) and we would "spread out" so that the Clerk couldn't watch us all. I remember Cody would first go down the Candy Aisle and get like 40 packs of

Beef Jerky and stuff them in his Jacket (Oh, I forgot to say that Cody would wear a "Trench Coat" even if it was summer) and then he would get a bunch of Candy, whatever kind we all liked. Next he would go over to the "Cooler" (the doors with the Beer and Soda inside) and would grab like 3-4 40 ounce Beers (usually Malt Liquor so we could get buzzed faster with less) and then we would make our way to the exit, never buying anything except maybe a pack of 25 cent "Juicy Fruit" if we had the quarter! We would then walk back about 200 yards to a Bridge Overpass where we would walk down the side of the hill leading under the bridge where we would sit and drink the beer and eat beef jerky while watching the cars go by. Then when we were done we would start walking back home Laughing at nothing but since we were "Buzzed" something was funny! Since we had to get by my parents (Cody's parents didn't give a shit if he drank) we would start eating all that "stolen candy" to cover our breath! It usually worked if we didn't do something stupid in front of our parents to let them know we were Buzzing! This happened at least 25 times at this store. But our "Borrowing" from stores went much bigger than this! This will be explained in another story!

CHRISTMAS CASH

Like I said before, we never had any real money (except when I would mow peoples lawns in the neighborhood for $2.50 and we would spend that on candy and cokes as soon as we got it) so we were always looking for ways to make money. Well, in the beginning and I'm not sure exactly who had the idea first, but I think it was my brother Terry, who thought "selling Mistletoe" door to door was a great idea. I must say, we did sell a lot of it that first year! We would go down to some river bottoms (a place that had a ton of trees with Mistletoe in them) and we would climb up trees and throw down as much mistletoe as we could get to, Garbage Bags full! We would "bag it up" in little sandwich bags and sell them for .50 cents apiece. People thought this was the cutest thing, we just thought about the money! The only problem was, we looked up to all our older brothers and just loved to go anywhere with them so when "Terry" and one of his friends offered to drive us around to sell the Mistletoe, we thought this was awesome! However, we didn't realize that there was a catch. We had to give all our money from selling the Mistletoe to our Brother so that He and His Friend could "Party" and then they would buy us a small Pizza somewhere cheap to make it seem "Worthwhile" to us! Needless to say, this only happened that first year, after that we went out on our own! The next year was o.k. but now it seemed like other people were selling it and giving us competition so we didn't make that much! We needed a new plan for raising "Christmas Cash" and we found it!

We would go "Christmas Caroling" (door to door) for our Church! We would turn a Coffee Can into a "Donation Can" with the Name of our Church on the outside and some "God Bless You's" written on it as well! When people asked we just told them that we were collecting for our church and that all the money was turned in every Sunday at Mass! This worked pretty good except for the fact that we had like (6) of us total that we had to split the money between so we had to do a ton of houses to make any money! If people closed the door in our face or gave us nothing and they had Christmas Lights up, we would swing back around and unscrew a bunch of lights and then throw them at the house and run, we sure fixed them! This was supposed to be Christmas time and people were supposed to "Give" didn't they realize this? Looking back on it now We do feel guilty for not turning in the money to our Church but we feel like we are even because not only did our parents put money in the "offering" every week but we also had to sit through long, very long sermons every week. Not to mention "Midnight Mass on Christmas Eve! This reminds me...I gotta go to Confession!!

YOU WILL HEAR A BELL

When I was about (8) years old I got into "Stealing" pretty bad! I would go to the store and steal candy, if I saw something I wanted in class at school I would take it. I would take money out of my Mom's purse, etc. In fact in 5th Grade I stayed after school one day (Detention) and as I was serving my Detention a kid took a nasty fall outside our classroom and my Teacher had to leave to take this kid to the office to see the Nurse. While she was gone I decided to snoop in her Desk and I found Her Purse! I was able to find a $10.00 dollar bill (which I took) before she got back. The only other kid in the class was my friend "John" who saw the whole thing but promised me he wouldn't say anything! I went home that night with my $10 bucks and I decided to tell my Brother Terry about it! I told him if he took me to the store and let me buy a candy bar and a soda, I would give him the rest (about $9.25, hey IT WAS 1980) so he could "Party!"

The next day when I got to class my teacher was pissed! She told the class   how she was driving home yesterday and stopped for gas. She said she "Pumped" $10.00 worth of gas because she new she had a $10.00 Bill. After she pumped the Gas and went to pay for it she couldn't find it anywhere! She knew she had it because she even saw it in her purse at lunchtime. She had already pumped the Gas so she had to call her Husband to bring her $10.00 and they lived in the hills, quite a ways away. She questioned everyone and decided that my friend "John" did it (he was the one In detention with me) and he got called to the principal's office. Well, he wasn't going to take the rap for me so he turned me in and I broke down during questioning and admitted it! My Dad (who was also a teacher at a different school in the District) got called at school and had to come to my school and pay my teacher back! Boy was I in trouble. My Dad was one of the Parents who signed the consent form saying "YES, YOU CAN SPANK MY CHILD IF HE GETS IN TROUBLE" (this was before corporal punishment was outlawed at school) so not only did the Principal give me a couple of "Hard Ass Spanks" but when I got home my Dad got his turn with the Paddle! Damn I was hurting!

Both My Mom and Dad decided that my stealing was getting out of hand and that I needed to go see a "Psychiatrist" about my problem. My Mom had a Mental Illness (she was Bi-Polar) and she saw a Doctor at Mental Health. She was able to get me seen ASAP! After my second appointment with this "Quack" he decided that I needed to be "Hypnotized" into not stealing and that anytime I felt the urge to steal, I would hear a loud Bell and this would tell me not to steal! A bunch of Bullshit! Anyway, the Doctor had a little medallion on a chain and he did the whole "You're getting sleepy routine" and I was getting sleepy but His Breathe was SO bad that every time I got a whiff, I would wake back up (but I kept my eyes closed the whole time) and this lasted like 10 minutes. I convinced Him that I was cured and my parents were skeptical but wanted to believe it! I was such a con artist that I had them believing this for a long time but eventually they saw right through that! Especially my Dad, He never bought it for one minute! One thing that changed was now I let "Cody" do the stealing and I was just the "Lookout" for undercover cops and store workers! Much safer doing my job!

"A BIKE TRIP TO TOWN"

As usual none of us had any Money, but that wasn't going to stop us from having fun on this Saturday! It was like 10:30am and we were rounding up all the guys (Cody, Joe, Jack, Ronald and of course Dan and I) to see what we wanted to go do. None of us had to be back until Dinnertime so we had like (6) hours to kill. We decided that we would ride our bikes up to the Mall and then we would ride into Marysville and then Yuba City. On our way to the mall there was this little "Greasy Spoon" called "The Shack # 2" and nobody knew where "The Shack #1" was and it was a good thing because you didn't need 2 of these places around! This place was typical "White Trash." When the old men would come in for coffee, they would help themselves and just throw the money into this basket sitting on the counter. It never got rang up; they just trusted you (see...White Trash!) Anyway, this place was funny because if you ordered a "Large Fry" to eat there, they gave you a pretty good size basket of fries, but if you ordered it to go…They would take a "Beer Flat" (the cardboard box that (4) six-packs of soda or beer comes in and line it with a piece of waxed paper and then just load the whole box full! It probably added up to like (3) of the large fries that they give you if you eat there! Well, like I said we had no money and I think the fries cost like .95 cents (this was like 1980-81) so when we would order the fries, we would act like we were digging the change out of our pockets while the old lady would go drop the fries into the grease. While she wasn't looking "Cody" would grab a bunch of change out of the "Coffee Basket" and we would be in business!! We would take the fries outside and everyone would just start grabbing handfuls with the grease just dripping down our arms, SO GOOD!!

Next it was off to the Mall. But with no money it wasn't that fun. We would go to "Flipper Flapper" which was the Arcade and we would all pretend like different games "ate" our tokens so the attendant would have to give us free ones but that only worked once. Soon after we would start to ride to Marysville, but on the way we would stop at "The Peach Tree Restaurant" to use the bathroom. If we were lucky, we would pass by a table where there was still a "Tip" and if no one was looking we would take it! That would buy us sodas or something later! Well when we got to Marysville we decided to go to "Ellis Lake" (A lake in the middle of town) and try to run over some ducks! We never could though because they were way to fast! Plus, some of the bigger Ducks would scare the hell out of us the way they would stop and size you up and then start coming at you while they "Hissed" and had that razor sharp tongue (looked like a tongue anyway) they were NOT scared of us at all! Except...JOE! He wasn't scared of the ducks, in fact he would find one of those "hissing" big ones and grab their long neck in the middle and just start "Wringing its neck" while the duck was honking and hissing and making all kinds of noise! We would laugh so hard, one of those laughs where you can't stop and your stomach hurts, you can barely catch your breath, a full bodied laugh! God it was funny!!

We then decided to ride into Yuba City (this was about 30-35 miles round trip from our houses) and go check out the Bowling Alley. We were sure to wear our "Oldest" and most messed up tennis shoes that day. We went up to the counter and told them we wanted a lane and what size shoes we needed. You had to give them your shoes in return for their rental shoes and then you just paid for them at the end of bowling when you paid for however many games you bowled! So, we probably played like (2) games each because when you have (5) bowlers on one lane, it takes a while. Oh yeah, we would do stupid stuff while bowling like someone would get up to bowl and roll the ball down the lane next to us (The people would get pissed) or we would roll the ball down our lane and when the "gate" would close to get the downed pins, someone would roll another ball and it would crash into the gate! We would "almost" get kicked out every time we bowled! Well, at the end of Bowling (we still had no money) one by one we would walk past the counter and go to the bathroom, and then we would slip outside to our bikes and be gone! We would all meet up a couple blocks from the bowling alley, still wearing our beautiful Bowling Shoes!!

By this time we had just enough time to ride back home before Dinner where we would eat like we never ate before!! Typical Saturday for us "White Trash!"

"SHOOTING BEERS"

We aren't sure if you know what "shooting" or "Shotgunning" Beers is so I will give you the definition: It's where you take an unopened beer (can) and turn it on its side, then you take a key or knife and puncture the can (making sure you don't spill a bunch of beer out) then you make about a 1- 2 inch hole at the bottom of the can. Everyone we have ever watched "shoot" a beer only puts a hole the size of a width of a pencil in the can. Way too small, it takes forever to finish the beer! When you're ready you put the beer up to your mouth with your lips all around the hole, then you tilt it "right side up" next you pop the beer open and all the beer comes rushing down into your mouth! You also need to burp right after or you might get sick!

We would always time it! To this day "Cody" still holds the record in Shooting Beers! I think his best time is like 1.95 seconds . Incredible! I've never seen anybody do it faster! We have won a lot of bets with people at parties who think Cody couldn't do it faster than like 3-4 seconds. I would go first (just to show people that I could only get like a 4 second time, just to sucker them in before Cody took over and then we would win their money but I had to have Dan or Cody open my cans because I would always make my holes "Jagged" so when I got done shooting my beer I would go to pull the empty can away from my mouth but it would get caught like a Fish on a hook! Painful!

I remember one Sunday Dan and I were on our way to Church (that our Dad and Mom made us go to every Sunday) and we were going to the 9:00am Mass because our Parents always went to the 10:30 one. They would always ask us who the Priest was (just so they could make sure we went to mass and didn't just skip it and go somewhere else) so we finally got smart and we would "Ro-Sham-Bo" (Rock, Paper, Scissor) to see who would have to sneak up to the front doors and peak inside to see who the priest was and to grab a "bulletin" to take home. We were sly!!

Anyway, one Sunday morning after seeing who the priest was, we went to a store and Dan didn't want to drink but I did, so I bought a six pack of Coors Light and a bag of "Funyuns" and we drove out to some Orchard off Live Oak Blvd. It was early in the morning and it was kind of hard to drink but I guess I wanted to impress my Little Brother so I had him make me a hole in my first beer so I could "Shoot" it. He got the watch ready and I slammed the first Beer in like 3.5 seconds. Decent time but I got disqualified because I "Threw up!" I couldn't hold the Beer down. Dan was laughing his ass off! I said, "That's o.k. I got 5 left!" Then I opened the bag of "Funyuns" and ate a few to get my stomach right! I told Dan to make me another hole and He was like "Are you sure?" I said "C'mon Smartass" I could do this easily! So...same thing happened, I opened it, slammed it and then threw up! Dan was in tears from laughing so hard! I don't know if I'm stubborn or just plain Stupid (probably a little of both) but I finished the six pack the same way as I started, I shotgunned everyone! I don't think I earned a "Buzz" because I still threw up, but I DID get a little buzzed!

Since we never had any money (or very little) we would always buy (or have someone buy for us since we were underage) some "Cheap" 12 pack of Beer. The one we drank the most was "Milwaukee's Best" it tasted the most like Coors Light, the beer we liked the best when we could afford it or if someone else was buying!!

"CAN WE GET A RIDE"

One rainy night we were over at a friend named Daryl's house. It was Me, Dan, Jack, Joe and Cody. We saw this ad in the paper for 6 packs of Soda for only .50 cents (limit 2) and this was one of the rare times that we all had a few bucks! The problem was the sale was at Longs Drugstore (in the Peach Tree Mall) and we didn't even want to pedal that far in the rain and at night as well. Well, Daryl's Brother "Chris" was home and so was their mom's car (an old beat-up Cadillac that was as big as a boat) and their Mom was gone to Bingo and wouldn't be home until late. So we "Bribed" Chris with a 6-pack of soda (we all chipped in .10 cents) to take us to Longs in the mall. Well we got there, everyone got their limit of 2 six packs of soda and we were off! On the way home Chris was "showing off" a little, I guess to try and impress us or something (didn't work though we just thought he was a lame ass) and decided that He needed to "jump" something in his Mom's Car! So we drove down this one street that had a railroad crossing that ran across it and it sloped up to the tracks and then back down. Like I said it was raining and the roads were already slick but "Captain Chris" thought he could "punch it" the 100 yards to the sloping track and somehow we would get "air" as our car would fly off the slope like in the "Dukes of Hazard." So he revved up the engine on this piece of shit and took off! I got to admit that it felt like we were going fast as hell! We braced for impact, hit the tracks, got like zero air and suddenly we started spinning out of control! Next thing I know we are busting through a barb wire fence into someone's property where they raise cattle and sheep! The Car was all smashed up but we were all fine! Chris and Daryl kept saying, "We are Dead, We are Dead." and it probably didn't help that we were all saying things like, "We told you that you shouldn't take the car without permission" or "Man, I wouldn't want to be in your shoes right now!" This pissed the two brothers off even worse but it WAS funny! We only had to walk about ½ mile to our houses so it wasn't that bad!!

We found out the next day that when Daryl and Chris' Mom got home from Bingo she asked the boys where her Car was and they both acted surprised and said they didn't know so She called the Cops and reported Her car stolen! Well guess what? They found her car about ½ mile down the road in some field and it looked like someone was horse playing because it had broken through a fence and there were skid marks all over the road! The Mom never found out the truth and we had fun threatening to tell on the Brothers for "stealing" the car! Damn, that was a funny time! Teach them to do us a favor!

"MAY I TAKE YOUR ORDER"

I had a friend "Doyle" who lived across the street from us and he worked at a Fast Food Place "Taco Charly" in Marysville. I remember I always use to bug him about getting me a job there. I would ask him all the time. I really bugged him! So one day he comes home and says, "Tomorrow at 4:00pm be ready to go and dress nice" and I'm like, "where we going" and he says "I got you an Interview with my Boss you Asshole and you better not blow it!" Boy was I nervous! I wondered if I got to eat all that delicious food for free or what? How much would I get paid, like $20.00 every hour? I was about to be a rich man!

So the next day Doyle takes me to "Taco Charly" and I meet his Boss "Suzie." She looks like a White lady but as soon as she started to talk, she had a huge accent! I think she was Chinese or Japanese or something. She was really kind of hard to understand so I would just Nod a lot and smile and say "yeah" when I didn't understand. She told me that the only reason she was giving me a chance was because I was friends with Doyle and how good of a worker

Doyle was! Shit, I didn't care what got me the job; I just wanted to make some money.

Suzie told me that I was starting out at "Minimum Wage" which was $3.35 every hour and that I would start out working like 20 hours a week! Man, I was in the money! That was like $65.00 a week! Awesome, I was going to be Rich!! It wasn't $20.00 an hour but it was close!

On the way home I thanked Doyle over and over again and said if you need anything just let me know! So Doyle says for the first (2) months he needs half my paychecks for getting him the job! I didn't really like this but what the Hell, he did get me the Job. I found out later that he was just screwing with me; he didn't want any of my money after all! Dick! ☺

After I had been there for a couple months I saw how things worked. Like if someone ordered a beef burrito no onions, but we accidentally made it WITH onions, we would wrap it up and put it in the "walk-in" (cooler). After your shift was over you could take home any of the mistakes. They were just going to throw them out anyway! We could eat for free before and after work. I got sick of this food pretty quick since I was eating it all the time! Well, I got pretty comfortable working there and I started "Dicking off" and playing around a lot, I was really immature and didn't know when to stop! So...I eventually got fired! However, I had another friend "Betty" who was a Supervisor at "Hillbillies" and she got me a job there about 1 week after I was let go from Taco Gong." After I had been there for about (2) months (I got in real good with the Manager, she loved me) I was able to get my Friend "Cody" a job there! Big Mistake! I made sure he only "cooked" and didn't do the Cash Register because I can guarantee Money would have been missing right away. This was "Cody" we are talking about!

We actually had a little money now since we were working part time but we didn't want to spend it on "fast food" where we worked (we still had to buy beer) so as usual we came up with a plan! Working at this Fast Food place you got 50% off your meals. This still wasn't good enough for us, so we gave ourselves a "Bigger Discount." Cody would come up and order from me, and he would order the smallest (and cheapest) burger we sold and the smallest fries as well. We already got free drinks. I would ring it up and it would come to like .72 cents (with the 50% discount) and the order would print out in the back for the "Cooks" to start making it. Cody would make it himself because we were slow and didn't have that many people working. The thing is…He would make like a 3 or 4 patty burger with about a pound of bacon and he would make like a full basket of fries! Workers had to eat in the back (there was a small break room with a table and 2 chairs) so he would gorge himself by eating all this food as fast as he could so nobody (like the Manager) could check his receipt and see that he was supposed to have the Kid Burger and fries and not this meal for 5 that he was choking down! You should have seen the Breakfast he would make for us! Like 3 pound omelets with Bacon, sausage, ham and anything else we wanted for like .50 cents! And we didn't even sell omelets! No wonder I had to keep buying bigger pants!

Cody eventually got fired for something I can't remember and I quit a short time later! Those were the days!

"TALES FROM THE DRIVE INN"

ONE OF THE FUNNEST THINGS I REMEMBER FROM GROWING UP WAS GOING TO THE DRIVE INN! I REMEMBER OUR PARENTS LOADING US UP INTO THE CAR, THROWING THE LAWN CHAIRS IN THE TRUNK AND GRABBING SOME BLANKETS. I REMEMBER MY MOM POPPING A TON OF POPCORN (ENOUGH TO FILL UP A PAPER GROCERY BAG!) WE COULDN'T AFFORD TO BUY THE "REAL STUFF" AT THE MOVIES! I CAN'T REMEMBER BUT I'M SURE WE TOOK ALONG SOME "GENERIC" SODA. IF WE COULDN'T AFFORD THE POPCORN THEN THERES NO WAY IN HELL WE WERE BUYING "COKES!" IT WOULD BE A WARM SUMMER NIGHT AND YOU WOULD PULL INTO A SPACE, HOPING THAT THE SPEAKER YOU GOT WORKED GOOD OR

YOU WOULD HAVE TO MOVE! WE WOULD GET THE LAWN CHAIRS OUT AND SIT IN FRONT OF THE CAR WHILE MY PARENTS STAYED INSIDE. IT WAS THE BEST! SO MUCH "WHITE TRASH" IN ONE PLACE, IT WAS AMAZING! IT WAS FUNNY TO SEE THE TEENAGERS PARK THERE CAR AND THEN OPEN THE TRUNK AND LET A FEW OF THEIR FRIENDS OUT. THIS WAS WAY BEFORE THE "$5.00 A CARLOAD" DAYS. YOU PAID BY THE PERSON! IT WAS FUNNY AT INTERMISSION BETWEEN MOVIES TOO. NOT ONLY DID THEY PLAY FUNNY ADVERTISEMENTS ABOUT BUYING FOOD AT THE SNACK BAR, LIKE THER HOTDOG JUMPING INTO THE BUN BUT WHEN YOU WENT TO USE THE BATHROOM THERE WAS USUALLY A GOOD FIGHT GOING ON OR SOMEONE'S DAD WOULD BE ALL DRUNK AND HE WOULKD COME OUT OF THE BATHROOM HAVING PISSED ALL OVER HIMSELF. IT WAS GREAT!

NOW FAST FORWARD LIKE 8-10 YEARS LATER…

THE DRIVE INN! STILL "NOT" $5.00 A CARLOAD YET (THIS CAME WAY LATER, BEFORE THEY FINALLY CLOSED THE DRIVE INN DOWN) SO WE TOO WOULD "SNEAK" PEOPLE IN THE TRUNK! HOWEVER, WE WOULD MAKE THE GUYS STAY IN THE TRUNK FOR LIKE 10 MINUTES AFTER WE PARKED, WHAT ASSES WE WERE! WINE COOLERS WERE THE BIG THING AT THE TIME. BARTLES AND JAMES WERE GOOD! I KNOW THEY WERE CONSIDERED ONLY FOR GIRLS BUT THEY WERE GOOD! YOU COULD SLAM A BOTTLE IN LIKE ONE DRINK! DRINK ENOUGH OF THEM AND YOU COULD GET BUZZED! I HEARD ANYWAY, I WAS A "GUY" SO I ONLY DRANK BEER! YEAH, RIGHT!

I REMEMBER ONE WILD NIGHT WE HAD. WE HAD A FRIEND NAME "RICO" (HE WAS MEXICAN TRASH

NOT WHITE TRASH LIKE US) AND HE WAS A FEW YEARS OLDER BUT HE WAS ONE OF THOSE GUYS THAT JUST HAD YOUNGER FRIENDS, PLUS HE HAD A FAKE I.D. SO HE COULD BUY BEER! I REMEMBER THERE WAS LIKE 5 OF US THAT WERE GOING OUT THAT NIGHT. WE ALL GOT AS MUCH MONEY AS WE COULD AND GAVE IT TO RICO. WE TOLD HIM TO BUY AS MUCH BEER AS HE COULD. WE TOLD HIM TO GET ICE TOO. WE ASKED HIM IF HE HAD ANY ICE CHESTS WE COULD USE AND HE JUST LAUGHED AND SAID HE HAD IT COVERED! WHATEVER HE MEANT BY THAT I DO NOT KNOW? BUT ANYWAY, WE ALL WENT HOME TO GET READY AND WE WERE GOING TO MEET AT RICO'S IN LIKE 2 HOURS. WE WERE GOING TO GO TO THE DRIVE INN, DRINK SOME BEER AND TRY TO PICK UP SOME GIRLS. GOOD PLAN! SO WE ALL GET OVER TO RICO'S AND WE SEE "NO BEER!" WE ARE ALL LOOKING IN HIS CAR, AROUND HIS HOUSE, NO BEER! WE ARE PISSED BECAUSE IF HE DIDN'T GET IT YET, WE ARE GONNA HAVE TO WAIT FOR IT TO GET COLD! SO RICO COMES OUT AND WE ARE LIKE, "DUDE, WHERE'S THE BEER?" HE GETS A SAD LOOK ON HIS FACE AND SAYS, I COULDN'T FIND ANY ICE CHESTS!" I'M LIKE, "YOU SAID YOU HAD IT COVERED, ESE!" THROWING IN THE "MEXICAN SLANG" ON HIM! HE THEN GETS A BIG ASS SMILE AND SAYS, "LOOK IN THE TRUNK PUTO!" SO WE GO OVER TO HIS CAR, HE OPENS THE TRUNK AND THE WHOLE THING IS FULL OF NOTHING BUT BEER AND ICE! IT'S LIKE THE WORLDS BIGGEST ICE CHEST! IT WAS BEAUTIFUL! WE HUGGED THE SHIT OUT OF HIM! THERE WAS OVER 100 BEERS! ACTUALLY IT WAS (5) CASES SO THAST'S WHAT, LIKE 120 BEERS! DAMN! SO WE GET TO THE DRIVE INN AND WE HAD TO PAY FULL PRICE, SEEING HOW WE COULDN'T HIDE IN THE TRUNK! WE START DRINKING A LITTLE BUT ARE BEING COOL BECAUSE WE ARE UNDERAGE AND DIDN'T WANT TO GET

BUSTED! SO IT GETS DARK AND THE FIRST MOVIE ENDS. WE GO UP TO THE SNACK BAR AND ARE "ON THE HUNT" FOR SOME GIRLS. WE KEEP RUNNING INTO FRIENDS FROM SCHOOL BUT WE COULDN'T TALK THAT MUCH, WE WERE ON A MISSION. NOW WE WENT TO LINDHURST, BUT SINCE THIS WAS THE ONLY DRIVE INN AROUND, KIDS FROM MARYSVILLE AND YUBA CITY CAME HERE TOO. WE RAN INTO THESE (3) GIRLS FROM MARYSVILLE HIGHSCHOOL WHO WERE CUTE. WE START TALKING TO THEM AND WE TELL THEM ABOUT THE "WORLDS BIGGEST ICE CHEST" AND THEY ARE LOVING IT. SO WE WALK THEM OVER TO THE CAR, SHOW THEM THE TRUNK AND IT'S ON. WELL, WE THOUGHT. THE NEXT MOVIE IS GETTING READY TO START SO THEY GET IN THE CAR AND WE ARE DRINKING. THEY ARE SLAMMING BEERS LIKE A DUDE, AND WE ARE LIKE, "WHAT'S UP?" SO CODY TRIES TO KISS ONE OF THE GIRLS AND GETS "SLAPPED!" KNOWING CODY, THAT'S NOT GOOD! HE SAY'S, "WHY YOU SLAPPING ME BITCH?" THEN ONE OF HER FRIENDS GETS PISSED AND IS LIKE, "WHO YOU CALLING BITCH" YOU UGLY PIECE OF SHIT! UH OH, IT'S ON! SO THERY START MAKING A SCENE, THREATNING US WITH GETTING THERE BROTHERS TO KICK OUR ASS, CALLING THE COPS, ETC. SO WE DECIDE TO LEAVE.

WE GO UPTOWN TO THE "CRUISE" AND WE SEE SOME GIRLS FROM LINDHURST STANDING IN FRONT OF JACK IN THE BOX. WE PULL OVER AND THEY ARE ALREADY BUZZING HARD! WE SHOW THEM THE "TRUNK" AND THEY ARE SO EXCITED!! THEY START BEGGING US TO TAKE THEM WITH US SO WHAT COULD WE DO, SAY NO? I DON'T THINK SO. THERE WAS 5 OF US AND 3 OF THEM, GOOD ENOUGH! UNLIKE THE LAST GIRLS, CODY WAS ALREADY MAKING OUT BEFORE WE GOT 2 BLOCKS AWAY! THIS WAS MORE

LIKE IT. WE DECIDE TO GO TO "AFRICA" AND PARTY. GOOD THING RICO BOUGHT CANS AND NOT BOTTLES BECAUSE WE TAUGHT THE GIRLS HOW TO "SHOTGUN" BEERS AND THEY WERE ACTUALLY FAST LEARNERS. NOW I DON'T WANT TO SAY THAT THESE GIRLS WERE "EASY" BUT LET'S JUST SAY THEY WERE VERY VERY "FRIENDLY" AND THEY APPRECIATED THE BEER. WERE THEY "GREAT LOOKING?" TO TELL YOU THE TRUTH, WE ALL HAD "BEER GOGGLES" ON SO YES; THEY WERE THE MOST BEAUTIFUL (AND WELL BUILT) GIRLS WE HAD EVER SEEN IN OUR LIFE! THEY WERE VERY FUN! I MUST SAY, I HAVE "NEVER" HAD A NIGHT QUITE LIKE THAT ONE EVER AGAIN. WHEN WE WOULD SEE THOSE GIRLS AT SCHOOL WE WOULD SMILE AT THEM, MAYBE WINK, BUT WE NEVER TALKED ABOUT IT. THEY RAN WITH A DIFFERENT CROWD. THERE FRIENDS PROBABLY WOULDN'T APPROVE! SO, JUST LIKE LAS VEGAS...."WHAT HAPPENS AT AFRICA, STAYS AT AFRICA!"

"PLACE YOUR BETS"

I think I was in Sixth Grade when Cody and I introduced "Gambling" to Yuba Gardens Middle School! We offered (2) games, the first was "Pitching Pennies" (which we used quarters) and the second was "Odds or Evens." The first game, "Pitching Quarters" you would stand back about (5-6) feet facing a wall and you would take turns to see who could get the closest to the wall. You could NOT roll the quarter up to the wall that was cheating! You had to just "flip" it and whoever got closest won. There was no limit on the amount of players but usually it was like 3-4. A lot of times it might just be you and one other. In the other game, Odds or Evens" you and another person would "Flip" your own quarter and catch it (like you were doing a coin toss) but making sure the other person did NOT see what you had, a head or a tail. Then you would take turns calling out either ODDS (if you thought the other guy had the opposite of you)or EVEN (if you thought the other guy had the same as you) you could look at your own coin!

It started off harmless enough; people would be playing it at recess in the Bathrooms or out on the blacktop. As word got around it started to get big! You would walk by a Classroom and the kids would be playing "Odds or Evens" while the teacher was writing on the Blackboard! They had so many kids going to the office asking for change (Quarters from their lunch money) when kids got desperate for quarters Cody and I would bring a $10.00 roll of quarters to school and make change at (3) quarters for a dollar! They were getting ripped off but they wanted to play so bad! See, Gambling is addictive!! I'd say after about a month of this it got out of control! They had the Principal come around to each class and lecture everyone on Gambling. They told us if we got caught, we would get "Spanked" (if your parents signed the Permission Slip saying that the School COULD spank your child) as my luck would go, My Dad DID sign it, saying "Hell Yes" spank my child and then I will too when he gets home. This was when "Corporal Punishment" was still legal. You would also get suspended for 1-2 days. The Gambling pretty much stopped but there were still some "Die Hard" players. Like this kid we called "Froggy" because he sounded like the kid "Froggy" from the "Our Gang" TV shows. Froggy would see me or Cody in the Halls and he would yell over, "Hey Dude, wanna Pitch? Odds or Evens? But the way his voice sounded you almost fell down laughing every time. I wish I could do the voice for you, you would crack up! Anyway, needless to say, I got busted Pitching Quarters in the bathroom one day and got sent to the Principal! First I got the Lecture, then I got the, "Isn't your Dad a Teacher?" Then it was "Swat" time. I always hated how they would say, "O.K. grab your ankles!" Then with a huge smile on their face...Crack! Then they would make you sit down just to rub it in. They would call my Mom and have her come pick me up. Then I waited for my Dad, hoping he would forget all about it, yeah right! Guess what? "Swat" time again! Usually He only did it once, and I would put on a good show of crying like I was dying! To Be Honest, what hurt most was letting My Mom and Dad "Down!" Whenever they were disappointed in me it hurt. Worse than 100 Swats! My Dad could just give you that "look of Disappointment" and it would make you feel terrible! So why did I keep on getting in trouble through the years and have to see that same look of disappointment you ask? Because I was an Idiot! I craved attention so bad! I would do anything (almost anything) to get a laugh!

"PLAY BALL"

Baseball was a big deal to us and our friends growing up and we all played Little League together! In fact, our friends "Joe and Jack Johnson" were on our team as well. We were all on the "Hippos" and our Coach was Mr. Eastman and his son John was on the team too. He was a pretty cool coach. Well, until I found out the only reason they picked me to be on the Hippos was to get my brother Dan! The league kind of "made" you take Siblings, to make it easier for the parents. This way they only had one Practice to take the kids to, one game for the parents to sit through, etc.

Dan was great at Baseball (every other sport as well) He made "All-Stars" every year (I went swimming) and He did great on those teams as well! Granted, I wasn't that good but I tried hard! I was however "Scared" of the Ball! Whenever I would get up to bat, I would stand in the right place, take good practice swings and kick the dirt a little (like the Pros) but as soon as the Pitcher would pitch the ball I would "step back" away from the plate or the ball or both. In fact, at every practice when I would get up to take "Batting

Practice" the Coach would line up like 8 bats "Behind" me so if I stepped back I would step on a bat or two and fall on my Ass! Needless to say I would have a very sore ass after every practice! Now I would swing mind you, but since I was "Away" from the plate I seldom made contact with the ball! And when I did, it was probably just luck and I probably had my eyes closed! No, the best thing that could happen for me and the team in a game was if I just went ahead and got "walked" or "Hit" by a Pitch so I could take my base! By the way..."John" (the Coach's Son) "stepped out" of the Batter's Box as well and he got the "Bat Behind You" treatment at Practice as well!

If there was one person known for getting "hit" by the ball it would be Jack Johnson! Man did he ever get hit by a pitch...almost every game if not twice a game! And his Brother Joe was o.k. but mostly just a "Legend in his OWN mind!" Speaking of the "Johnson's," the funniest part of the games was when Mrs. Johnson would show up to watch the game, with Her "Megaphone!" She would park out in Right Field behind the fence and get settled in, and then the "Fun" would begin! She would be all "Shit-Faced" from Pre-game Cocktails and would start yelling while playing "Charge" on her Megaphone and would just be having way too much fun! Whenever Dan or I or one of her sons would be announced next to bat on the P.A. System she would yell, "WOOH, WOOH, WOOH, WOOH" let's get something going! C'mon "Michael" or C'mon "Danny Boy" let's get a Goddamn hit! "WHOO, WHOO, WHOO, WHOO." I know it embarrassed the Shit out of Joe and Jack but what could they do? Everyone loved it!

Even to this day, when anyone brings up playing Baseball when we were younger, one of the first things that come up is Mrs. Johnson and her "WOOH, WHOO, WHOO'S." Mrs. Johnson was a "Baseball Legend" as much as "Mickey Mantle" or "Babe Ruth" ever was! May She "Rest in Peace!"

"MARCIA, MARCIA, MARCIA"

Growing up, we lived in a small "Cul de sac" and everybody knew everybody! Well, one day this new family moved in and it looked like they had kids our age. Come to find out that one of the girls (Trixie) was my age, the 2nd Daughter (Marcia) was Dan's age and then there was a son (Bucky) who was a year or two younger. Anyway, they kept to themselves for a while until one day "Marcia" was Roller Skating on the sidewalk in front of our house and she was going really fast. She could turn backwards while skating and then do 360 Degree turns. She was really good. Well this day, while skating in front of our house (Dan and I were bagging the grass that we just mowed) she tried to do some "Spin" move but her skate must have hit a rock or something because when she came down she

"Ate Shit" but good! I know it had to hurt but it was just too damn funny so Dan and I just started laughing! She got up, dusted herself off and said, "What's so "F-ing" funny? We just looked at her and I said, "Oh nothing, my Brother just told me a Good Joke!" We didn't want to hurt her feelings since she just moved here and didn't know anybody. So She says, "What's the Joke, I want to hear it!" Well, we didn't have a joke so we just lied and said, "We can't tell you it because it's pretty Dirty!" She then say's, "Yeah, that's what I thought, Chicken Shits!" Oh Hell No, now it was on! We turned on the hose and drenched the shit out of her, she was so mad we thought her Red Hair was going to catch fire! She had Red Hair and "Freckles" all over and you could tell she was tough! She was going to fit in good around us! Her Sister "Trixie" on the other hand was Blonde, Skinny and shy! Who cares what their brother looked like, right? Anyway, after that Marcia was always coming over bugging us and trying to mess up our "Street Football" games or our "Wiffle Ball" games we played in the street as well. She would chase down a foul ball and then try to run away with the ball, or try and trip us when we were running with the ball, just all kinds of "Stupid Shit!" Always trying to get attention! I don't think she got hugged enough growing up? She sure use to "piss us off!" Especially if we were losing!

I'm not sure who ever started this but after a while (Months) we got to know Marcia pretty well and we would always shove her around or throw Her down into a bush or something while she roller-skated, stuff like that. She loved the attention and would basically bug us until we did "slam" her or throw her down! Like I said, she loved it! And still to this day, she is the "Toughest" girl I have ever seen! She could take a beating!! She endured all kinds of beatings from us! We would start out playing "tag" or something and when we tagged Her it was more like a full on "blow to the Back" slap or something, I mean you could hear it down the street and she would just smile and say, "Is that all you got you Pussy?" Then we would have Wrestling Matches and she would say before the match, "Mike, I know you, Dan and Jack are going to kick my ass but at least I know it will be close between Joe and I!" Joe hated this shit because we would "Taunt" the hell out of Joe saying how he would always get his ass kicked by a girl, how a girl could whip his ass, etc! And honestly, it was close! I'm not sure if she just got "UP" more when she battled Joe or what but it was some "Body Hurting Laughter" to witness this to be sure! SO FUNNY!!

I Can remember things like Marcia running down the street and someone throwing a heavy fiberglass tube at her legs, making her trip (while running full blast) and just "Skidding" down the street in shorts! I remember Marcia getting grabbed by the hair and having her face get drug along a "cyclone" fence! Jack Johnson while wrestling her one time got her in a "Figure Four Leg Lock" and "popped" her Knee cap out of joint. Painful! She just went home, told Her parents she fell and went to the hospital! That was one thing about Marcia, she would NEVER tell her Parents on us! No matter how bad she got it, she always took the blame! I know it sounds terrible and it probably wasn't the best thing we should have been doing but She loved the attention, could take a punch (and give one, just ask Joe) and well after all... We were "Growing up White Trash!"

Last thing, we always said Marcia would be awesome in the Army because she could "kick some Ass" and guess where she went after graduating High School? YEP, the ARMY! She's definitely an "Army of One!"

"IF THE TRAILER'S A-ROCKING, DON'T COME A-KNOCKING!"

The Johnson's had this white, beat-up old trailer that was parked in their Driveway, "unfixable!" It looked like it slept (4) about 15 years ago. It was a mess! However, to us kids it was awesome!

It started out as just a place to "Hang Out" However; it quickly became our "Make Out Headquarters" as we were getting older, but not necessarily more mature! We would mess around and get someone to buy us some Beer and then we would drink the Beer as fast as we could (since we only got about 3 or 4 Beers each we figured whoever could drink them the fastest was the "MAN") and we could use being "Buzzed" for the reason we were "making out" with "Beauty Challenged Girls" or

Girls that weren't really LARGE but were just "Big Boned!" Sometimes we would even get "Lucky" and the girl we were making out with would still have "most" her teeth! Usually though, they had "Horse Breathe", smoked Cigarettes with NO filters and had teeth the color of a "Highlighter!" That's REALLY yellow for you people who didn't get the joke!

Mrs. Johnson HATED to have anyone in the trailer! She hated to have anyone in the House either! She wanted to get drunk in Peace! Now if she was "Already" Buzzing hard when we got there and was in a good mood, well that's another story! She would have you come in and sit on down at the Dinner table then She would make you Eat whatever GROSS thing She made for Dinner! I guess it was Edible since Joe and Jack ate it. However, I was just thinking back and those two DID miss a lot of School! Mrs. Johnson wouldn't take NO for an answer! She was always saying or yelling, EAT IT! EAT IT! Even when Dan and I would "Lie" and say we were allergic to something (just so we wouldn't have to Eat It) she would think about it for like 2 seconds and then say, "OH HORSESHIT" you're not Allergic! Jack would plead with his Mom to just let us go without eating but she was persistent! We would wait until she turned around to "scrape" up whatever concoction she had made and then Dan and I would make a run for it! Oh, that would REALLY Piss her off!! All we could hope for was that she would forget by the next day! It usually worked!

The Trailer was fun but it was "Scary" as well! I remember sometimes being in the trailer "Making Out" with a girl when all of a sudden you would hear... "Who's Out There?" and "I'm Coming in to Get You!" It was Mrs. Johnson, Drunk off her ass! Thank god she didn't know how to open the trailer! We could lock it good from the inside! Still scary though! In the back of your mind you wondered if this was going to be the night she finally was able to open it! The girls would be scared! They would be hugging us tight and shaking! Shit, I was shaking too! I needed the "Girls" to hold me!! I couldn't wait for Mrs. J to go in the house for another beer so we could make a break for it!!

There was no Electricity to it, so it was always dark! Sometimes you would take a girl into the "Love Shack" and suddenly you would smell something bad! You never knew if you were going to "sit in something" left behind either! GROSS! It was embarrassing! We just didn't have many options! Too young to drive so we didn't have a car to go "park" in. We couldn't take the girls to our house because our parents wouldn't let us just go back to our room with a girl! Sometimes we would go to the school but a lot of girls couldn't "jump the Fence" so that was out! No, we HAD to take advantage of the trailer, as gross as it was! Needless to say, we usually didn't get the same girl to visit the trailer twice!

A few months later they decided to get rid of the trailer! It was a bittersweet day. On one hand we were sad to see it go. We had a lot of memories in that nasty trailer! In fact, some of you girls reading this right now may have experienced it. I'm sure you wouldn't admit it though. I can't blame you! On the other hand, it served its purpose and it was time to put it "out of its misery!" White Trash at its best!

"LOOK UP IN THE AIR, IT'S A BIRD, IT'S A PLANE, NO IT'S... WATER BALLOONS"

WE HAD ANOTHER GAME WE LIKED TO PLAY AND AT THE TIME WE THOUGHT IT WAS FUNNY AS HELL, HOWEVER AS WE GOT OLDER AND STARTED TO DRIVE IT DIDN'T SEEM AS FUNNY. BUT LOOKING BACK NOW, IT STILL WAS FUNNY!! IT STARTED OUT WITH US (JOE, JACK, CODY, DAN AND MIKE) DRINKING UNDER AN OVERPASS OF A BRIDGE. IT WAS A COOL PLACE TO DRINK BECAUSE NOBODY CROSSING THE BRIDGE ABOVE US KNEW WE WERE DOWN THERE AND ANY CARS DRIVING UNDER THE OVERPASS (LIKE THE CHP) WOULD BE

TRAVELING WAY TOO FAST TO STOP AND IF ONE DID COME BY WE WOULD SIMPLY RUN BACK UP TOP TO THIS TRAIL BEHIND A BUNCH OF HOUSES (YOU COULDN'T DRIVE BACK THERE) AND FINISH DRINKING THERE. ANYWAY, BACK TO BEING UNDER THE BRIDGE! SO, DRINKING UNDER THE OVERPASS WAS COOL FOR AWHILE BUT LIKE ANYTHING ELSE, IT GOT BORING. SO I CAN'T REMEMBER WHO HAD THE IDEA BUT WE DECIDED TO MAKE "WATER BALLOONS" AND THROW THEM AT CARS DRIVING BY. WE WOULD TAKE A BUCKET OF "PRE-MADE" WATER BALLOONS UNDER THE OVERPASS (WE WERE LUCKY ONLY 1-2 WOULD BREAK ON THE WAY) AND GET READY FOR "WAR!" WE WERE NOT VERY GOOD AT FIRST, BUT WE GOT BETTER! WE WOULD GO 1 AT A TIME, UP ON THE OVERPASS, GET READY AND "KABOOM" "SPLAT" RIGHT ON THEIR WINDSHIELD! TIMING WAS EVERYTHING! AND BOY DID THE PEOPLE GET PISSED SOMETIMES! THEY WOULD STOP THEIR CAR, GET OUT AND CURSE AT US WHILE WE WOULD BE LAUGHING AND FLIPPING THEM THE BIRD! OTHER TIMES THEY WOULD JUST BRAKE A LITTLE AND KEEP DRIVING, WE ALWAYS WONDERED IF THEY THOUGHT THEY HIT A BIRD OR SOMETHING? WE STOPPED DOING THIS FOR AWHILE AS IT GOT A LITTLE BORING UNTIL WE MET "THE DEVIL'S OWN!" THIS WAS A "PAPER MACHE" W/ HEAVY TAPE REPLICA OF THE HIGH SCHOOL'S MASCOT "A DEVIL!"

THE SCHOOL JUST PLAYED ITS LAST FOOTBALL GAME OF THE SEASON AND THE MASCOT CAME OFF A HALFTIME FLOAT AND THEY WERE JUST THROWING IT AWAY, STUPID ADULTS!! WE JUST SCORED THIS BIG FIND! SO WE TOOK OUR "LIFE SIZE DEVIL" TO OUR OVERPASS AND WE TIED ROPES TO IT AND THEN WE TESTED IT, READY TO GO! AS SOON AS A CAR WAS IN OUR LANE WE WOULD THROW IT OVER AND THE DEVIL WOULD JUST ABOUT HIT THE WINDSHIELD AND THEN WE WOULD "YANK" IT UP! THIS WAS WAY MORE FUN THAN THE WATER BALLOONS BUT MORE DANGEROUS TOO! O.K. O.K. KIDS DO STUPID THINGS SOMETIMES! IN OUR CASE, A LOT!

WE DID THIS FOR A FEW WEEKS UNTIL WE ALMOST GOT CAUGHT ABOUT 10 TIMES! THAT WAS "ALMOST" BECAUSE WE NEVER _ACTUALLY_ GOT CAUGHT!

AFTER THIS GOT BORING WE WERE LOOKING FOR SOMETHING ELSE TO DO. ONE THING WE LIKED TO DO WAS WALK ON THE "OUTSIDE" OF THE CHAIN LINK FENCE THAT WAS ABOUT 8-10 FEET TALL THAT WAS ATTACHED TO THE GUARDRAIL AND PROTECTED PEOPLE WALKING ACROSS THE BRIDGE. WE WOULD GO DOWN TO ONE END OF THE BRIDGE WHERE THE FENCE BEGAN AND WOULD START WALKING SIDEWAYS ON THE "OUTSIDE" OF THE FENCE! THE ONLY THING SEPERATING US FROM THE CARS SPEEDING BELOW WAS THE GOOD 75-100 FOOT DROP! IT WASN'T TOO BAD UNTIL YOU GOT

ABOUT HALF WAY ACROSS AND REALIZED YOU ALREADY WENT TOO FAR TO TURN AROUND (PLUS YOU DIDN'T WANT TO BE CALLED A PUSSY BY YOUR PALS) AND YOUR FINGERS STARTED CRAMPING UP FROM GRIPPING THE FENCE SO HARD WHILE HANGING ON FOR DEAR LIFE! NEEDLESS TO SAY, THAT GOT OLD REALLY FAST! PLUS, IM SURE MORE THAN ONE OF US LEFT SOME "SKID MARKS" IN OUR UNDERWEAR FOR "MOM" TO FIND IN THE HAMPER! AFTER THAT, I DON'T REMEMBER WHOSE IDEA IT WAS BUT IT WAS A GOOD ONE! THE OVERPASS (BRIDGE) HAD THESE REALLY TALL HILLS HOLDING IT UP (LIKE GRASSY HILLS) AND IT WAS STEEP! WE WOULD FIND SOME CARDBOARD AND THEN SIT DOWN ON IT AT THE TOP OF THE HILL, THEN SOMEONE WOULD GIVE YOU A "PUSH" AND YOU WOULD FLY DOWN THIS HILL WITH THE GRASS ACTING AS A "SLIP & SLIDE" UNTIL YOU CAME TO REST AT THE BOTTOM, WHICH WAS ONLY ABOUT 1-2 FEET FROM A CAR IF IT WAS COMING DOWN THE FREEWAY AT THE SAME TIME. AND TRUST ME; WE HAD SOME "CLOSE CALLS." THIS WAS FUN FOR A LITTLE WHILE BUT I THINK WE QUIT DOING IT BECAUSE WE WOULD "DRINK" A LITTLE BIT AND BE TOO LAZY TO WALK ALL THE WAY UP THE HILL AGAIN AND THEN REPEAT IT. WE SAID "THE HELL WITH THAT!"

GRUMPY'S TAVERN (OLIVEHURST'S ONLY BAR)

WE HAD THIS POOL HALL/WHITE TRASH BAR WHERE WE LIVED AND FOR SOME REASONS KIDS WERE ALLOWED IN THIS PLACE YOU JUST COULDN'T DRINK UNLESS YOU WERE 21(NOW I'M NOT SAYING WE DID OR WE DIDN'T) AND THEY SERVED ALL KINDS OF PEOPLE!

WE JUST WENT THERE TO PLAY VIDEO GAMES AND POOL! I THINK IT WAS STILL .25 A GAME AND THAT WAS THE BEST DEAL IN TOWN, ESPECIALLY SINCE IT WAS THE "ONLY DEAL IN TOWN!" WE

USED TO THINK WE WERE SOME REAL "BADASSES" AND "POOL SHARKS" EVEN THOUGH WE HAD TO USE THE BAR'S POOL CUES, WHICH WERE ALL "BEAT TO HELL" AND CROOKED MOST WERE MISSING THE TIPS, VERY WHITE TRASH!

ALWAYS LOOKING FOR A WAY TO MAKE A BUCK, CODY AND I FIGURED OUT THAT WHEN THE BARTENDER'S BACK WAS TURNED WE COULD TAKE THOSE BIG, NEON BEER SIGNS THAT PLUG IN! SOME OF THESE WERE REALLY COOL AND YOU COULD HANG THEM IN YOUR BEDROOM OR SELL THEM TO SOME WHITE TRASH HICK THAT WOULD HANG EM IN THEIR GARAGE AND PRETEND THEY HAD A NIGHTCLUB! THEY WERE COOL...NOT! WE NEVER GOT CAUGHT BUT WE GOT DAMN CLOSE!!

ANOTHER TIME THE BARTENDER FROM GRUMPY'S WAS SAVING ALUMINUM CANS IN THIS _HUGE BOX_ AND WE DECIDED HE DIDN'T NEED THEM ANYMORE SO ONE NIGHT AT ABOUT 9:00PM WE RODE OUR BIKES OVER TO GRUMPY'S AND THE PLACE WAS ROCKING, WELL...ABOUT AS MUCH AS A PLACE COULD ROCK WITH TOOTHLESS GUYS WHO WORE DIRTY CLOTHES AND STUNK, TO THE GIRL HO'S WHO WOULD SLEEP WITH YOU IF YOU BOUGHT THEM A BEER, LIKE A "NATURAL LIGHT" OR WHATEVER WAS CHEAPEST AT THE TIME. ANYWAY, THIS BIG BOX OF CANS WAS OUT BACK AND WE HAD TO SNEAK BECAUSE THE MENS BATHROOM WAS IN BACK TOO! WE WOULD WALK QUITELY

OVER TO THE BOX AND START FILLING UP OUR TRASH BAGS WITH THESE CANS AND WE WERE DOING A PRETTY GOOD JOB OF IT UNTIL WE HEARD THIS HUGE DOG BARKING AT US! WE STILL WANTED TO MAKE MONEY JUST NOT IN A WAY THAT GET'S US BIT! WE DIDN'T KNOW THAT "GRUMPY'S" EVEN HAD A DOG! OH WELL, WE WENT BACK TO THINKING UP MORE IDEAS!

"IT'S GONNA TAKE MORE THAN A COAT OF PAINT TO MAKE IT AT THUNDER ROAD" (FROM THE MOVIE "GREASE")

"THUNDER ROAD"

AT OUR HIGHSCHOOL (LINDHURST) WE HAD THIS LONG "SEMI-PAVED" ROAD THAT LED FROM THE MAIN STREET ALL THE WAY TO THE STUDENT PARKING LOT (ABOUT 300 YARDS) AND IT WASN'T IN THE BEST OF SHAPE BUT IT "DID" HAVE SPEED BUMPS!

ANYWAY, THERE WAS THIS GIRL, RED HAIR, FAKE LEATHER JACKET AND SHE WAS ABOUT 5 FOOT 2, WEIGHING IN AT 350+ WITH RED

FRECKLES! THIS WAS "SALLY-ANN." WE USED TO LOVE TO MESS WITH SALLY-ANN AT SCHOOL BECAUSE SHE WOULD PLAY ALONG AND MESS WITH US AS WELL! OH, I FORGOT....SALLY-ANN DROVE A MOTORCYCLE TO SCHOOL AND IT WAS A PIECE OF SHIT, SOME KIND OF YAMAHA. WELL, SHE LOVED THIS PIECE AND I MYSELF RODE A RED HONDA 250 "REBEL" WHICH I LOVED BECAUSE IT WAS SO FUN AND I COULD RIDE IT AROUND FOR PRACTICALY NOTHING! ANYWAY, ONE DAY SALLY-ANN CAME UP TO ME (SCARED THE SHIT OUT OF ME) AND SAID,"HEY MIKE I HEARD YOUR LITTLE KIDDIE MOTORCYCLE CAN BARELY MAKE IT OVER THE SPEED BUMPS AND THAT YOU WANTED TO MAYBE "PULL OUT" OF OUR LITTLE RACE?" I NEVER LAUGHED SO HARD IN MY LIFE! ME PULL OUT? I DON'T THINK SO!! I FORGOT TO MENTION THAT I BET SALLY-ANN THAT I COULD TOTALLY "BLOW HER AWAY" IN A SHORT MOTORCYCLE RACE! SHE HAPPENED TO BE AROUND HER 2 FRIENDS AND DIDN'T WANT TO LOOK BAD SO SHE ACCEPTED THE BET!

I LAUGHED AGAIN AND SAID,"SALLY-ANN" I CAN'T WAIT UNTIL THIS IS OVER, COLLECT MY $2.00 "AND NO PENNY ROLLS, I WANT DOLLAR BILLS" AND TO EVEN MAKE IT EASIER FOR YOU I DECIDED TO HAVE "CODY" ON THE BACK OF MY BIKE. THIS MIGHT GET US CLOSER TO YOUR WEIGHT BUT YOU WILL STILL OUTWEIGH US! SHE JUST SAID,"F-YOU PUNKS, I WILL SEE YOU AT 2:45PM AT THUNDER ROAD AND DON'T TRY NO FUNNY STUFF!"

CODY AND I WENT UP TO HER TO SHAKE HANDS BUT AS SOON AS SHE PUT OUT HER HAND WE BOTH SLAPPED THE SHIT OUT OF HER BACK (SHE WAS WEARING HER EVERYDAY FAKE LEATHER JACKET)AND YOU COULD HER THAT SLAP THROUGHOUT THE SCHOOL! SHE GOT SO PISSED AND TURNED BRIGHT RED AND SHE TRIED TO RUN AFTER US UNTIL SHE GOT "WINDED" AFTER ABOUT 10 SECONDS. SHE SAYS,"SCREW THIS, I'M GOING TO SAVE MY ENERGY FOR THE RACE" AND WE SAID,"GOOD LUCK HOT MAMA WE'LL SEE YA AT THUNDER ROAD!

WELL THE BELL JUST SOUNDED AND I HAD TO WAIT FOR CODY TO GET OUT OF HIS REMEDIAL READING CLASS. CODY SHOWS UP ALREADY LAUGHING AS WAS I AND WE WENT AND GOT MY BIKE AND CRUISED IT AROUND THE STUDENT PARKING LOT. I GUESS EVERYONE HEARD ABOUT OUR RACE BECAUSE NOBODY WAS LEAVING, WHICH WAS FINE WITH ME I JUST DIDN'T WANT ANY TEACHERS AROUND TRYING TO STOP IT, ALTHOUGH I'M SURE THEY WOULD LAUGH THEIR ASS OFF AS WELL! WE WAITED ABOUT 10 MINUTES UNTIL MY COMPETITION FINALLY SHOWED UP AND I SAID,"WOW I'M IMPRESSED; I DIDN'T THINK YOU WERE GOING TO SHOW UP!" SHE SAYS,"SSSHHHIIITTT, I WOULDN'T MISS THIS FER NUTING, Y'ALL GOIN TO GET Y'ALL ASS KICKED UP IN HERE!" SHE MUST HAVE HAD SOME STRONG

COFFEE OR SOMETHING BECAUSE SHE WAS ON FIRE!

WE GOT LINED UP AT THE STARTING POINT NEXT TO OUR LOVELY COMPETITION AND WE HAD SOMEONE COUNT DOWN FROM 3 TO GO! BAM, WE WERE OFF, WE TOOK THE LEAD INSTANTLY, HER BIKE STARTED TO EMIT BLACK SMOKE. WE WERE DOING WHEELIES OVER THE SPEED BUMPS AND I SWEAR I COULD HAVE DID A 360 TURN AND STILL BE AHEAD! WE SLOWED TO A STOP UNTIL SHE COULD CATCH UP THEN WE TOOK OFF FOR THE FINISH LINE AND IN SECONDS WE CROSSED THE LINE AND WON THIS HUGE RACE! SALLY- ANN CAME CREEPING UP ON HER BIKE WITH HER HEAD DOWN AND RESTING ALL HER CHINS ON HER CHEST! I ACTUALLY FELT SORRY FOR HER, NOT CODY THOUGH! HE WAS LIKE,"BITCH WE WON, BITCH WE WON, LET'S HAVE THE MONEY, LET'S HAVE THE CASH-OLA!! SO SALLY-ANN REACHED INTO HER 74 INCH (WAIST) LEVIS AND PULLED OUT TWO OF THE MOST TORE UP DOLLARS YOU EVER SAW. SHE THEN LOOKS AT ME (SHE'S IGNORING CODY BY NOW) AND SAYS,"I THINK I GOT A DIRTY CARBEURTOR AND A COUPLE ADJUSTMENTS TO MAKE" SHE THEN GIVES ME THE "WHITE MAN HANDSHAKE" (THAT'S WHERE WHEN SOMEONE COMES UP TO YOU AND SAYS "HI" AND KINDA LIFTS HIS HEAD UP AND THEN BACK DOWN (LIKE A NOD) QUICKLY TO SIGNIFY "WHAT'S UP?") AND SAY'S "DAMN GOOD RACE" THEN PUTS HER HAND OUT TO SHAKE. I WAS VERY, VERY

HESATANT TO DO THIS BECAUSE SHE COULD STILL HAVE FOOD ON HER FINGERS OR SHE COULD PULL ME IN AND GET ME IN THE "SLEEPER HOLD" ANYTHING! WELL, I SHOOK HER HAND (QUICKLY) AND MOVED BACK, WHEN ALL OF A SUDDEN, OUT OF NOWHERE, I HEAR THIS LOUD "SMACK" IT WAS CODY SLAPPING THE SHIT OUT OF SALLY-ANN'S BACK! I JUST GOT ON MY BIKE, CODY JUMPED ON BACK AND WE DROVE OFF FASTER THAN SHIT, JUST LAUGHING SO HARD I THOUGHT I WAS GOING TO WRECK. I HAD TO PULL OVER. THIS STORY MIGHT SOUND FUNNY, BUT IF YOU HAD WITNESSED IT, YOU WOULD HAVE TO SAY IT WAS THE FUNNIEST THING YOU EVER SAW!

WE NEVER RACED AGAIN, ALTHOUGH WE OFFERED PLENTY OF TIMES. CODY WAS LOOKING OVER HIS SHOULDER FOR THE REST OF THE SCHOOL YEAR BECAUSE SALLY-ANN PROMISED TO GET HIM BACK, BUT IT NEVER HAPPENED. FUNNY STORY THOUGH, HUH?

"WHEN THE FAIR COMES TO YOUR TOWN"

EVERY YEAR AROUND THE END OF AUGUST THE COUNTY FAIR WOULD ROLL INTO TOWN. WE WERE LUCKY IF WE GOT TO GO ONCE (THE FAIR WAS OPEN FOR 5 DAYS ALWAYS ENDING ON A SUNDAY AND WE WERE STILL ON SUMMER VACATION) WHILE IT WAS HERE! THE FAIR WAS THE SAME EVERY YEAR... YOU HAD CARNIES (A CARNY WAS A RIDE OPERATOR OR A GAME OPERATOR AND THERE WAS ONLY 2 REQUIREMENTS YOU HAD TO HAVE TO GET HIRED...MISSING OR "JACKED UP" TEETH AND LOOK AND/OR SMELL DIRTY OR FUNKY! THERE WERE SOME SCARY LOOKING DUDES WORKING THESE RIDES! THE SAME GUYS YOU TRUSTED TO PUT TOGETHER THESE RIDES! MISSING BOLTS, SCREWS? DIDN'T MATTER...NOTHING DUCT TAPE CAN'T FIX!

OUR LUCK CHANGED ONE YEAR AND I CAN'T REMEMBER WHO TOLD US THAT MR. KISERROLL NEEDED VOLUNTEERS TO SELL COKES IN THE GRANDSTAND EVERY YEAR, DURING THE RODEO, DEMOLITION DERBY, CONCERTS,ETC. WE DIDN'T GET PAID FOR DOING THIS BUT WE GOT OUR NAMES ON THE LIST AT THE FRONT GATE GETTING US IN FREE, AS MUCH PEPSI AS WE WANTED AND AN OPPORTUNITY TO GET IN BEFORE ANYONE ELSE COULD AND BE ABLE TO WALK AROUND THE FAIR AND DICK WITH THE CARNIES BEFORE WE HAD TO GO TO THE GRANDSTAND TO HELP OUT. ONE OF THE FUNNIEST THINGS WAS THE WAY JOE WOULD MESS WITH THE CARNIES. WE WOULD BE WALKING BY ONE OF THE GAMES AND THE CARNY WOULD SAY,"C'MON BIG GUY YOU CAN DO THIS, THIS IS AS EASY AS PIE! THEN JOE WOULD SAY,"I'LL PLAY YOUR GAME IF YOU CAN SHOW ME YOUR "DENTAL RECORD." THEY WOULD GET SO PISSED AND SOMETIMES EVEN JUMP OUT OF THERE AND CHASE HIM DOWN! ANOTHER ONE THAT WAS FUNNY,SOMEONE WOULD TAKE JOE'S SLEEVE AND WALK HIM UP TO THE GAME. THE GAME WAS THE ONE WHERE EVERYONE GETS A SQUIRT GUN AND YOU SPRAY THE WATER INTO THE CLOWNS MOUTH AND IT WOULD BLOW UP A BALLOON AND THE FASTEST PERSON GOT A PRIZE. THE FUNNY PART WAS JOE WOULD GET THE SQUIRT GUN CLOSEST TO THE CARNY AND WHEN THE BELL SOUNDED, JOE WOULD "DRENCH" THE CARNY WITH WATER AND

WE WOULD ALL JUMP IN FRONT OF JOE AND TELL THE CARNY THAT HE WAS BLIND AND HE DIDN'T MEAN TO DO IT. WHAT WAS THIS ANOREXIC-WANNA BE HARLEY RIDER GONNA DO? HE NEEDED THIS JOB! IT'S NOT TOO MANY PLACES THAT WOULD HIRE THIS "ONE TOOTH SMELLY GUY WITH TATOOS ON HIS FORARMS THAT READ,"F---THE WORLD" AND ON THE OTHER HE HAD A NAKED LADY WITH "MY OLD LADY IS A BITCH!" I ASSUME ONLY THE COUNTRY FAIRS!

WHEN AFTERNOON/NIGHT CAME WE GOT READY TO WORK! WE WOULD ALL GO TO THE GRANDSTAND AREA AND START FILLING UP CUPS OF COKE AND SPRITE. THEN WHEN THE STANDS STARTED "FILLING UP" WE WENT TO WORK! I USUALLY TOOK JACK WITH ME AND FOR GOOD REASON! HE WOULD YELL,"COKES, GET YOUR COKES HERE!" THEN HE WOULD ALSO CARRY THE "TRAY" WITH ALL THE COKES ON IT! ALL I HAD TO DO WAS MAKE CHANGE AND HAND OUT COKES! I'M SURE JACK DIDN'T LIKE THIS MUCH AND WANTED TO "TRADE OFF" BECAUSE CARRYING ALL THOSE COKES UP AND DOWN THE GRANDSTAND STEPS GETS TIRING AND OLD QUICK, HOWEVER I WOULD JUST KEEP HIM MOTIVATED AND TELL HIM, "JUST THINK OF ALL THAT MUSCLE YOU ARE GONNA GET!" THEN HE WOULD JUST GIVE ME A GREAT BIG GOOFY SMILE AND SAY, "YEAH....YOUR RIGHT MIKE!"

AT THE END OF THE NIGHT YOU WOULD TURN IN YOUR "SMOCK", YOUR CHANGE AND ANY MONEY YOU MADE ON THAT LAST NIGHT. WE WOULD THEN GET A RIDE HOME WITH A RANDOM PERSON AND THEN IT WAS "OFF TO BED" TO DREAM ABOUT GIRLS" AND BE PREPARED FOR THE NEXT DAY!

WE GOT PRETTY SAD WHEN THE FAIR WAS OVER BECAUSE NOW WE HAD TO FIND OTHER WAYS TO SPEND OUR TIME! BACK TO MOWING LAWNS, WASHING CARS (SOMETIMES WE WOULD WEAR OUR SEXIEST SHORTS (THE KIND THAT RIDE UP YO ASS) SO THAT WE WOULD GET MORE "TIPS!" DID IT HELP? I GUESS NOT BUT IT SURE DID GET A LOT OF LAUGHS! OH WELL, WE LOOK FORWARD TO NEXT YEAR!

"BO-BO COME INSIDE"

WE HAD A FRIEND NAMED "HENRY" WHO WENT BY THE NAME "BO-BO." HE WAS $\frac{1}{2}$ ASIAN AND $\frac{1}{2}$ WHITE TRASH. HIS MAMA-SAN WAS CHINESE OR JAPENESE OR "DIRTY KNEES...LOOK AT THESE!" ANYWAY, SHE WAS ASIAN AND HIS DAD WAS A FELLOW "WHITE TRASHER" LIKE US. HE HAD 1 BROTHER AND 1 SISTER (BOTH OLDER) AND THEY STAYED TO THEMSELVES PRETTY MUCH.

WE USED TO PLAY A LOT OF "TWO HAND TOUCH" FOOTBALL AND "WIFFLE OR SOCK BALL" ON OUR STREET (BO-BO LIVED AT THE END OF OUR STREET) UNTIL IT GOT DARK AND EVEN A LITTLE LATER THAN THAT. _EVERYNIGHT_ WHEN IT WOULD GET DARK, WITHOUT FAIL...BO-BO'S MOM WOULD COME TO THEIR DOOR AND YOU WOULD FIRST

HEAR A LOUD "WHISTLE" (LIKE COACH'S WEAR) AND WE WOULD KEEP PLAYING OR SAY,"BO, YOUR MOM'S CALLING" AND BO WOULD SAY,"IT'S O.K. KEEP PLAYING." THEN A COUPLE MINUTES WOULD PASS AND THEN YOU WOULD HEAR (AS LOUD AS BO'S MOM COULD YELL...BECAUSE SHE WAS A FRAGILE OLD LADY THAT WEIGHED LIKE 75 POUNDS) "BO-BO", COME INSIDE, DINNER A READY!" SOMETIMES BO WOULD SAY,"I'LL BE THERE IN 5 MINUTES" AND THEN SHE WOULD GET PISSED! I WOULDN'T SAY SHE WENT "APE SHIT" BUT SHE DID GET FIRED UP! SHE'D YELL "YOU COME INSIDE RIIGGHHTT NOWWW DINNER ARE A READY!" THEN SHE WOULD MUMBLE SOMETHING IN CHINESE AND SLAM THE DOOR!" DAMN, IT WAS FUNNY!

IT WAS ALMOST AS FUNNY AS THE TIME DAN AND I SPENT THE NIGHT AT BO'S (FIRST AND LAST TIME WE STAYED) AND HE HAD "SHOWTIME" ON HIS T.V. (HE WAS LUCKY-THIS WAS WHEN SHOWTIME JUST CAME OUT) AND WE WERE GOING TO WATCH "THE EXORCIST" AT LIKE MIDNIGHT! SO...WE WATCHED THE MOVIE AND THEN WENT TO BED. I SLEPT ON THED FLOOR AND DAN AND BO-BO SLEPT ON BO'S BED. WELL...DAN HAD NIGHTMARES THAT NIGHT ABOUT "THE EXORCIST" AND ENDED UP "THROWING UP" ALL OVER BO-BO! I THINK HE WOKE ME FIRSTAND IT WAS LIKE,"MIKE, MIKE, I GOT SICK." I SAID ARE YOU O.K.? "HE SAID YEAH, BUT I THINK I THREW UP ON "BO-BO!" IT WAS ONE OF THOSE THINGS THAT WAS SAD YET FUNNY AS

HELL! ON ONE HAND I FELT BAD FOR MY LITTLE BROTHER BUT ON THE OTHER HAND I THOUGHT IT WAS FUNNIER THAN SHIT THAT BO-BO GOT "SLIMED" BECAUSE IF IT WAS THE OTHER WAY AROUND, BO WOULD BE LAUGHING HIS ASS OFF AT US, GUARANTEED!!

BO-BO WAS A COOL GUY (MOST THE TIME) EXCEPT IF YOU NEEDED HIM TO BUY YOU BEER. BO-BO WAS LIKE 4 YEARS OLDER THAN US, AND WHENEVER WE WANTED HIM TO BUY US BEER-HE WOULD CHARGE US! IT MIGHT BE A COUPLE BUCKS TO FILL UP HIS MOTORCYCLE (WHICH WAS A NINJA....GO FIGURE) OR WE WOULD HAVE TO BUY HIM SOMETHING TO EAT LIKE A BUNCH OF "CHICKEN LITTLES" AKA "BAK BAK LITTLES" FROM KFC WHATEVER IT WAS IT WAS ALWAYS SOMETHING! AS A MATTER OF FACT, I REMEMBER HIM NOT BEING A GOOD SHARER FROM WAAAYYY BACK. IN THE SUMMER WE WALK DOWN TO THE LOCAL TRAILER COURT TO SNEAK IN AND GO SWIMMING (WHICH WE ALWAYS GOT CAUGHT AFTER LIKE 10-15 MINUTES) BUT I REMEMBER WALKING TO THE TRAILER COURT AND PICKING UP BO-BO ON THE WAY, HE'D BE EATING HIS CUP O' NOODLES WHICH COULD HAVE ONLY COST PENNIES BACK THEN SINCE THEY ARE SO CHEAP NOW! WOULD HE GIVE YOU A BITE? HELL NO, BECAUSE THERE WAS NOTHING IN IT FOR HIM! HE WAS LIKE THAT THOUGH! HIS DAD ON THE OTHER HAND WAS COOL AS HELL! TO BAD WE DIDN'T FIND THIS OUT

UNTIL MUCH LATER, WE COULD HAVE SAVED A LOT OF MONEY PAYING BO-BO! "TODD" WOULD BUY FOR US ANYTIME, HE JUST NEEDED A RIDE UP TO THE STORE. THEN WHEN WE GO BACK HE'D BE LIKE,"YOU GUYS WANNA COME IN HERE AND DRINK?" BEING THAT WE WERE ALWAYS LOOKING FOR PLACES TO DRINK AND NOT GET CAUGHT, WE WERE LIKE "HELL YEAH!" IN FACT A LOT OF TIMES TODD WOULD SAY,"YOU GUYS WANNA SMOKE A JOINT?" WE WERE LIKE YEAH, BONUS! BO-BO NEVER OFFERED ANYTHING LIKE THIS! HE MUST HAVE TOOK AFTER HIS MOTHER (FROM ALL THE TIMES HE HAD TO...."COME INSIDE") GOD BLESS HER SOUL!!

LAST I HEARD TODD HAD PASSED AWAY. HE WAS A "TRIP" AND WAS A VERY COOL DUDE! I THINK BO-BO IS A TEACHER SOMEWHERE DOWN SOUTH (L.A. MAYBE) AND I BET HE'S STILL NOT SHARING HIS "CUP O' NOODLES" WITH THE OTHER TEACHERS IN THE TEACHERS ROOM!

"GREASE"

WHEN I WAS IN THE 5TH GRADE THE MOVIE "GREASE" CAME OUT AND I THOUGHT THIS WAS THE BEST MOVIE I EVER SAW! IN FACT I THINK I SAW IT ABOUT 10-15 TIMES THAT YEAR. JOHN TRAVOLTA (DANNY) WAS "THE MAN" AND OLIVIA-NEWTON JOHN (SANDY) WAS THE MOST GORGEOUS WOMAN I HAD EVER SEEN!

WELL, I HAD A CRUSH ON THIS GIRL NAMED "BETTY." SHE HAD BLONDE HAIR AND A KILLER SMILE, THE KIND THAT MAKES YOU "MELT" WHEN THE SMILE IS FOR YOU! BETTY SHARED MY LOVE FOR GREASE AND SAW IT ABOUT AS MANY TIMES AS I DID. AT RECESS WE WOULD ACT OUT PARTS IN THE MOVIE, BECOMING "DANNY AND SANDY" TO THE DELIGHT OF OUR LOYAL FRIENDS FROM NOT ONLY OUR CLASS BUT 4TH AND 3RD GRADERS AS

WELL. WE DREW A PRETTY BIG CROWD. THE TEACHER THAT HAD "DUTY" WOULD ALWAYS THINK IT WAS A FIGHT!

I WILL NEVER FORGET THE DAY BETTY SHOWED UP TO SCHOOL WITH HER HAIR PERMED! SHE LOOKED JUST LIKE SANDY DID IN THE END OF THE MOVIE WHERE SHE AND CODY SING "I BETTER SHAPE UP." I COULDN'T WAIT UNTIL RECESS SO WE COULD ACT OUT THOSE PARTS! WELL RECESS CAME AND I WAS "WARMING UP" MY VOICE TO SING AND BETTY COMES UP TO ME AND SAYS,"MIKE, YOU KNOW I LIKE YOU RIGHT?" I SAY,"DON'T YOU MEAN DANNY ZUCCO?" SHE SAYS "NO, JUST MIKE." LISTEN, I MET THIS GUY WHO LIVES BY ME BUT HE GOES TO OLIVEHURST SCHOOL AND HE ASKED ME TO GO WITH HIM AND I SAID YES! PLUS, I'M GETTING KINDA TIRED OF THIS WHOLE "GREASE" THING,IT'S GETTING LAME! "I THOUGHT "YOU BITCH!" BUT I PLAYED IT OFF, I SAID I WAS ACTUALLY GETTING READY TO ASK THIS GIRL OUT WHO LIVED BY ME BUT DID "HOME SCHOOL" (I LIED) SO IT'S COOL! SHE SAID THE ONE THING WE GUYS ALWAYS HATE TO HEAR…."WE CAN STILL BE FRIENDS." I SAID "OH YEAH" NO PROBLEM! I SAID I HAD TO TAKE A LEAK AND I WENT TO THE BATHROOM AND CRIED MY EYES OUT, I LOVED THIS GIRL, I WAS READY TO MARRY HER AND BUY A HOUSE, HAVE KIDS, EVERYTHING! OH WELL? THIS WOULDN'T BE THE LAST TIME I HAD MY HEART BROKEN! AFTER THAT, ALL I WANTED TO SING WAS

"STRANDED AT THE DRIVE IN" AND I WOULD SIT ON THE SWINGS AND SING, "STRANDED AT THE PLAYGROUND" STRANDED A FOOL, WHAT WILL THEY SAY...MONDAY AT SCHOOL?! THIS WAS DEPRESSING! WE GOT A "NEW GIRL" A COUPLE DAYS LATER AND I REMEMBER ASKING HER IF SHE LIKED THE MOVIE "GREASE?" SHE SAID SHE DID. SHE HAD BLACK HAIR AND WAS KIND OF A LITTLE "SMARTASS!" SO I THOUGHT, WHAT IF I CHANGE THINGS AROUND AND I MAKE THE NEW GIRL "RIZZO" AND I JUST FALL FOR HER INSTEAD OF SANDY? THIS COULD WORK, RIGHT? WRONG! I RAN THIS PAST "RIZZO" AND SHE JUST LAUGHED AND STARTED CALLING ME "DANNY ZUCCHINI!" WHAT A BITCH! THIS PRETTY MUCH ENDED MY "GREASE" CAREER! THE FUNNY THING IS AFTER ALL THESE YEARS "SANDY" AND I HAVE RECONNECTED ON FACEBOOK AND SHE'S MY GOOD FRIEND! WE LAUGH AND JOKE ABOUT OUR "GREASE" ROLES NOW! I WONDER WHAT EVER HAPPENED TO "RIZZO?" THAT BITCH! ☺

"WOULD YOU LIKE YOUR LAWN MOWED?"

LIKE I WAS SAYING PREVIOUSLY, WE WERE ALWAYS BROKE (MY LITTLE BROTHER AND I) AND LOOKING FOR WAYS TO MAKE MONEY. I CAN'T REMEMBER HOW IT STARTED BUT I WOULD GO AROUND THE NEIGHBORHOOD PUSHING THIS "HEAVY ASS" LAWN MOWER AND A ONE GALLON GAS CAN. I PROBABLY SHOULD HAVE LEFT THESE AT HOME AND JUST WENT AND ASKED FIRST AND IF I GOT A JOB THEN GO GET THE MOWER. HOWEVER, I THOUGHT IF THEY SAW THE MOWER AND KNEW I WAS READY THEY MIGHT SAY YES. IT WORKED PRETTY GOOD. I CHARGED $2.50 FOR THE FRONT AND $2.50 FOR THE BACK. I HAD A BAG ON THE

MOWER SO I DIDN'T HAVE TO RAKE THE GRASS (THANK GOD) OR BAG IT UP. YOU WOULD ALWAYS GET SOME "CHEAP BASTARD" WHO WOULD WANT WAY MORE WORK THAN THE $2.50 WAS WORTH. I WOULD GET LIKE HALF THE LAWN MOWED AND THEN THEY WOULD COME OUT AND SAY,"CAN YOU LOWER IT, IT'S STILL TO LONG!" SO I WOULD HAVE TO START OVER AND THEN WHEN I WAS DONE THEY WOULD WANT ME TO SWEEP THE SIDEWALKS, STUFF LIKE THAT! I WOULD GET THEM BACK THOUGH, AT NIGHT I WOULD RIDE MY BIKE OVER TO THEIR HOUSE AND START "SKIDDING" ON THEIR GRASS AND RUNNING OVER SOME FLOWERS...I FIXED THEM ALRIGHT! MOST PEOPLE WERE COOL AND SOMETIMES THEY WOULD OFFER YOU A SODA OR THEY WOULD GIVE YOU LIKE $3.00 (.50 CENT TIP) SO THAT WAS COOL.

MY PROBLEM WAS, AS MY DAD WOULD SAY,"THAT MONEY IS BURNING A HOLE IN YOUR POCKETS!" I WOULD SPEND IT AS QUICK AS I GOT IT! I WAS, HOWEVER THE BEST SHARER AROUND. WHOEVER WAS AROUND ME (USUALLY MY LITTLE BRO DAN) WOULD GO UP TO "SHORTSTOP" AND GET SLURPEES AND PLAY PINBALL, EAT CANDY, ETC. THE MESSED UP THING WAS MY BROTHER DAN WOULD HAVE MONEY BUT HE WOULD *NEVER SPEND IT!* HE WOULD ALWAYS EAT AND DRINK MY STUFF BUT HE WOULD HOLD ON TO HIS AND ACT LIKE HE WAS BROKE! IT'S FUNNY NOW BECAUSE TODAY HE'S ONE OF THE MOST "GIVING" PEOPLE I KNOW!

ANOTHER ONE OF OUR GREAT "MONEY MAKING IDEAS" WAS TO SELL WATER "DOOR TO DOOR." BACK IN THE LATE 70'S THEIR WAS ALL THIS TALK ABOUT A WATER SHORTAGE AND HOW PEOPLE WOULD HAVE TO RATION WATER BECAUSE THEIR WOULD BE NONE. SO, NEEDLESS TO SAY WE WANTED TO HELP OUR NEIGHBORS AS WELL AS MAKE A FEW BUCKS AT THE SAME TIME! WE GOT A 5 GALLON BUCKET AND FILLED IT WITH WATER (THEIR WAS THINGS FLOATING IN IT) AND PULLED IT DOOR TO DOOR WITH OUR WAGON. WE COULDN'T UNDERSTAND WHY EVERYONE WOULD LAUGH AS WE ASKED IF THEY WANTED TO BUY SOME WATER BECAUSE OF THE SHORTAGE COMING. THEY WOULD ASK HOW MUCH? WE WOULD SAY LIKE .25 CENTS FOR A GLASS FULL AND LIKE $1.00 FOR THE WHOLE BUCKET OF WATER. WE DIDN'T GET VERY FAR, EXCEPT A COUPLE PEOPLE BOUGHT A GLASS FULL AND A COUPLE OF PEOPLE BOUGHT THE WHOLE BUCKET! WHEN SOMEONE MENTIONED THEY COULD JUST GET WATER OUT OF THEIR FAUCET WE KNEW WE WERE "GOING OUT OF BUSINESS!"

"YOU'RE GETTING SLEEPY"

MY "STEALING" HAD BEEN GETTING PRETTY BAD AS FAR AS TAKING MONEY FROM MY MOM'S PURSE OR TRYING TO GET INTO MY DAD'S WALLET WHEN HE WAS ASLEEP OR LITTLE THINGS FROM STORES. MY MOM SUFFERED FROM A BI-POLAR DISORDER AND SHE SAW A PSYCHIATRIST AT MENTAL HEALTH. WELL, SHE SPOKE TO HIM AND HE AGREED TO TRY AND HELP ME GET OVER ALL THIS "STEALING" THAT WAS GOING ON.

I MET DR. HOOCHIE ONE DAY AND HE SEEMED LIKE A NICE ENOUGH GUY. HE WAS ASIAN AND KINDA HARD TO UNDERSTAND BUT I MANAGED. HE ASKED ME THE TYPICAL QUESTIONS LIKE WHY DO

YOU TAKE IT? WHAT DO YOU DO WITH IT? HOW MUCH DO YOU TAKE? ETC.

ONE OF DR. HOOCHIE'S SPECIALTIES WAS "HYPNOTHERAPY" AND HE WANTED TO HYPNOTIZE ME SO THAT I WOULD NOT STEAL ANYMORE. HE HAD ME SIT UP ON THE COUCH AND HE PULLED UP A CHAIR. HE TOOK OUT SOME SORT OF "MEDAL" ON A GOLD CHAIN AND HAD ME WATCH IT GO BACK AND FORTH WHILE HE TOLD ME I WAS GETTING SLEEPY (JUST LIKE YOU SEE ON T.V.) AND I PLAYED ALONG. AFTER ABOUT 5 MINUTES HE WANTED ME TO LIE DOWN ON THE COUCH AND RELAX. HOWEVER, EVERY TIME HE SPOKE I WOULD GET A BIG WHIFF OF HIS BAD BREATH! I MEAN "KNOCKDOWN" BAD BREATH. I COULD NOT CONCENTRATE OR GET INTO IT, BUT I PLAYED ALONG. AT ONE POINT HE TOLD ME,"EVERYTIME YOU GET THE URGE TO STEAL SOMETHING YOU WILL HEAR A BELL AND THAT WILL REMIND YOU THAT YOU DON'T WANT TO STEAL ANYTHING ANYMORE! WELL, I WAS GLAD I MADE IT THROUGH THE SESSION WITHOUT THROWING UP FROM HIS BREATH.

I LET MY MOM AND DAD KNOW WHAT HAPPENED AND HOW THIS "BELL SOUND" WAS GOING TO CURE MY STEALING! MY MOM THOUGHT THIS WAS THE GREATEST THING EVER BUT MY DAD WAS REALLY SCEPTICAL AS HE SHOULD HAVE BEEN, IT DIDN'T WORK!! I DID QUIT TAKING MONEY FROM MY MOM AND DAD SO THEY FELT LIKE MAYBE IT

ACTUALLY WORKED! THE NEXT THING I WANTED TO STEAL WAS SOME LISTERINE FOR DR. HOOCHIES BAD BREATH!!

YOU NEED IT, WE CAN GET IT & "THE WHITE TRASH ROBIN HOOD"

CODY AND I MADE A GREAT TEAM WHEN IT CAME TO "BORROWING" THINGS FROM STORES; THE BAD THING ABOUT IT WAS WE NEVER RETURNED ANYTHING! LUCKILY WE NEVER GOT CAUGHT BORROWING THINGS.

IF YOU NEEDED SOMETHING AND THE PRICE WAS RIGHT WE COULD GET IT FOR YOU. ONE TIME

SOMEONE REALLY WANTED A LEATHER JACKET, BUT THEY DIDN'T WANT TO PAY WHAT THEY WERE GOING FOR, SO CODY AND I WENT DOWN TO THE DEPT. STORE AND LOOKED AT THE JACKETS. VERY NICE. ONLY ONE PROBLEM...THEY WERE CHAINED TO THE RACK SO NOBODY WOULD BORROW THEM ☺ SO WHAT DOES CODY DO? HE TAKES OUT SOME "BOLT CUTTERS" AND CUTS THE CHAIN, PUTS ON NOT ONE BUT TWO LEATHER JACKETS AND WALKS RIGHT OUT OF THE STORE! HE MADE US SOME MONEY AND GOT A LEATHER JACKET OUT OF THE DEAL. HE'S WALKED OUT OF A SPORTING GOODS STORE SWINGING A $100.00 TENNIS RACKET! WHEN THOSE CORDS THAT ATTACH TO YOUR SUNGLASSES AND LET YOU HANG THEM OFF YOUR NECK WERE POPULAR, WE WOULD GO TO A BIG STORE AND GRAB EVERY COLOR, LEATHER ONES ANYTHING! YOU NEED SUNGLASSES TO GO WITH THEM? NO PROBLEM!

I CALLED CODY THE "WHITE TRASH ROBIN HOOD" BECAUSE HE "STOLE FROM THE RICH" THIS BEING THE STORES AND HE "GAVE TO THE POOR" WELL, WE DID CHARGE A LITTLE BUT IT WAS JUST LIKE GIVING THE STUFF AWAY TO OUR FRIENDS AND OTHER "POOR WHITE TRASH " LIKE US. IT SEEMED LIKE AT ONE POINT, EVERYONE AROUND US WHO HAD SUNGLASSES, NEW SWEATERS, SHOES, ETC. HAD BENIFITED FROM OUR "SALES EVENTS!" "NICE JACKET!" WHERE DID YOU GET IT? OH, I SHOP AT "MIKE & CODY'S!"

CODY WAS DEFINITELY A PRO AT "BORROWING" THINGS FROM STORES! THE ONE TIME I TRY TO TAKE SOMETHING I GET BUSTED! I WAS IN A LONGS STORE AND MY "FAT-ASS" WAS CRAVING A SNICKERS CANDY BAR. BUT SURPRISE, I HAD NO MONEY! SO SINCE I HAD SEEN CODY DO THIS A MILLION TIMES I THOUGHT, "NO PROBLEM!" I PICK UP THE SNICKERS BAR, WALK AROUND THE STORE ACTING LIKE I WAS INTERESTED IN VITAMINS AND SHIT THEN OUT I GO. THIS STORE WAS INSIDE A MALL SO I WAS "SPEED WALKING" DOWN THE HALL LIKE A MAN ON A MISSION, WHEN I SPOTTED A MAN FOLLOWING ME AND HE WAS GETTING CLOSER! I MADE IT TO AN EXIT DOOR WHICH LED ME OUTSIDE AND I STARTED TO RUN, HOWEVER I WAS HUNGRY SO I RIPPED THE CANDY BAR OPEN, TOOK A HEALTHY BITE, AND TOSSED THE REST IN A FLOWER BED! ANYWAY THE MAN CAUGHT ME AND TOLD ME THAT HE KNEW I TOOK THE BAR OF CANDY AND HE JUST NEEDED TO GET MY PICTURE AND INFO AND HE WOULD LET ME GO! I ASKED IF HE WAS GOING TO CALL MY PARENTS AND HE SAID NO! AS LONG AS I COOPERATED (WHICH I DID FULLY) AND TOLD THE TRUTH! HOWEVER, THE BASTERD LIED!! HE LEFT FOR A MINUTE, CAME BACK AND SAID,"YOUR DAD IS ON HIS WAY HERE AND HE IS PISSED!" I SAID ,"YOU LIED!" AND HE JUST LAUGHED. WHAT A DICK! SO...MY DAD GETS THERE AND HE'S PISSED! HE HAS TO PAY FOR THE CANDY BAR AND THEN GET A LECTURE ON MY STEALING. THEN WE GOT TO GO HOME. HE WAS SO PISSED

AND I GOT LIKE 2 WEEKS RESTRICTION WITH CHORES TO PASS THE TIME! I BLEW IT! WORSE THAN THAT, I LET MY DAD DOWN AND I COULD TELL WHAT A "DISAPOINTMENT" I WAS TO HIM! THAT WAS WORSE THAN ANY PUNISHMENT I COULD HAVE GOT! WAS I EVER GONNA GROW UP AND BE A GOOD KID?

TONY THE TIGER

NOW I'M NOT SURE HOW WE ACTUALLY MET "TONY" BUT HE WAS A "TRIP!" TONY WAS A BLACK GUY THAT WASN'T ALL THERE. I THINK HE WAS JUST SLOW...REALLY SLOW. ANYWAY, TONY STUNK,BAD! HE LIVED WITH HIS OLDER BROTHER AND I ASSUME THE "STATE" PAID THEIR RENT. NO MOTHER NO FATHER, NOTHING. ANYWAY, WE WOULD GIVE TONY A FEW BUCKS HERE AND THERE TO HELP HIM OUT (MAYBE BUY SOME SOAP, DEODERANT,ETC) BUT THEN WE FOUND OUT HIS OLDER BROTHER WAS TAKING THE MONEY WE GAVE HIM! HE WAS A REAL ASSHOLE! SO WE JUST BOUGHT TONY THE SOAP AND STUFF OURSELVES. HE WOULD GO HOME, TAKE A SHOWER AND COMEBACK TO US FOR INSPECTION. IF HE STILL STUNK (THIS HAPPENED A LOT) HE WOULD GET

SENT BACK TO START OVER! ONCE HE WAS GOOD AND CLEAN WE WOULD TAKE HIM TO McDONALDS AND GET HIM FED. DRINKING (BEER) WAS ALWAYS GOING ON AS WE WERE BECOMING BIG TIME ALCOHOLICS! ONE THING WE USED TO LIKE TO DO WAS TAKE TONY WITH US TO WALGREENS AND THEY WOULD HAVE THIS BASKET OF WHISKEY OR TEQUILA, JUST NASTY "ROCK-GUT" STUFF ON CLEARANCE AND WE WOULD BUY US BEER AND TONY A BOTTLE OF WHATEVER! WE THEN TOLD TONY THAT IF HE DRANK THE WHOLE BOTTLE IN 15 MINUTES WE WOULD GIVE HIM $5.00 AND SINCE HE ALWAYS WANTED MONEY HE WOULD _ALWAYS_ TAKE THE CHALLENGE! HE WOULD USUALLY WIN THE BET TOO BUT HE WOULD BE SO HAMMERED HE'D FORGET ABOUT THE MONEY. THE FUNNIEST THING WAS HERE'S THIS GUY, IT'S 10:00 AM AND HIS WHOLE DAY IS SHOT BECAUSE HE'S DRUNK OFF HIS ASS! TOO FUNNY! HE ALWAYS USED TO SAY "OFF THE WALL" STUFF. ONE OF HIS FAVORITE THINGS TO SAY WHEN HE SAW A WOMEN (GOOD LOOKING OR NOT) WAS, "I WANNA CHOW OFF HER TITTIES AND EAT THEM LIKE WATERMELON!" HE SAID THAT ALL THE TIME! TONY WAS VERY RESPECTFUL THOUGH. HE ALWAYS ADDRESSED US AS MR. MIKE AND MR. CODY. HE EVEN WOULD SAY, "HOW YOU DOING MISS LISA?" NOT SURE WHERE HE GOT HIS MANNERS BUT IT WAS FUNNY TO HEAR! ONE TIME WE TOLD HIM WE HAD TO GO AND HE WAS "RIPPED" AND DIDN'T WANT US TO LEAVE SO WE TOLD HIM TO HANG ON TO THE SIDE OF

THIS BEETLE WE WERE DRIVING AND WE TOOK OFF WITH HIM HANGING ON FOR DEAR LIFE! HE ALMOST FELL LIKE (10) TIMES, TRUST ME IT WAS FUNNY! HE THEN GOT OFF AND STARTED WALKING IN THE PARK, FALLING DOWN, ETC. GOOD TIMES! WE MOVED FROM THESE APTS. AFTER ABOUT A YEAR AND I THOUGHT WE WOULD NEVER SEE TONY AGAIN! I RAN INTO TONY SEVERAL YEARS LATER AND HE DIDN'T REMEMBER ME AT ALL! I EXPLAINED THE THINGS WE USED TO DO, THE DRINKING, THE GOIUNG OUT TO EAT, HELL I EVEN MENTIONED THE "WATERMELON TITTIES" STILL HE REMEMBERED NOTHING! I ACTUALLY GOT KINDA SAD! I KNOIW WE USED TO HAVE A LOT OF FUN WITH TONY, BUT WE REALLY DID CARE ABOUT HIM! HE TOLD ME HE HAD MOVED IN WITH SOME NICE FAMILY AND WAS GOING TO CHURCH! I THOUGHT, "THAT'S AWESOME!" I WAS REALLY PROUD OF HIM FOR TURNING THINGS AROUND AND ADJUSTING SO WELL!

FREDDY

JACK AND JOE HAVE A BROTHER (HALF BROTHER) NAMED "FREDDY" AND WHEN HE WAS YOUNGER HE GOT INTO A BAD CAR ACCIDENT! WELL HE GOT ALL THESE PINS INSERTED INTO HIS NECK, LEGS, WRISTS, ALL OVER. OH YEAH, HE'S MENTALLY ILL AS WELL! ANYWAY, YOU WOULD SEE HIM WALKING DOWN THE STREET, STOP, AND ALL OF A SUDDEN HE WOULD START "CRACKING" HIS NECK FROM SIDE TO SIDE, BUT REAL VIOLENTALLY, THEN HE WOULD "CRACK" HIS LEG BACKWARDS (LIKE YOUR DOING A REVERSE FIELD GOAL) ABOUT 10 TIMES! FOR SOME REASON HE HAD A PASSION FOR "CAMOFLAUGE CLOTHING!" HE NEVER HAD ANYTHING TO DO WITH THE MILITARY BUT HE LOVED THEIR "CAMMIES!"

THE FUNNEST THING TO DO WAS TO GO UP TO HIM AND WHERE EVER YOU TOUCHED HIM,HE WOULD HAVE TO SLAP IT. THEN HE WOULD "CRACK IT" OUT! THIS NEVER GOT OLD!

FREDDY WAS ON SOME SORT OF DISABILITY AND HE WOULD GET A CHECK ON THE FIRST AND BY THE 3RD OR THE 4TH HE'D BE BROKE. HE WOULD ALWAYS BUY HIS NECESSATIES WHICH WERE, CIGARETTES, COFFEE AND "NO-DOZE." THEN. HE HAD A FETISH FOR JEWLERY. HE WOULD GO TO THE LOCAL "ARMY SURPLUS" AND BUY A RING FOR LIKE $35.00 - $60.00 AND THEN WHEN HE RAN OUT OF MONEY HE WOULD GO TO A PAWN SHOP AND SELL IT FOR LIKE $5.00 HE NEVER GRASPED THE IDEA OF MAYBE "NOT" BUYING RINGS AND STLL HAVING SOME MONEY LEFT OVER! HE NEVER LEARNED HIS LESSON! EVERY WEEK...NEW JEWLERY!! JUST ANOTHER
"BROKE RICO SUAVE!" EVERTIME "WE" SAW HIM WE'D SAY,"FREDDY, WHERES OUR MONEY DAMNIT!" HE'D BE LIKE,"I DON'T OWE YOU KNOW MONEY!" WE'D SAY,"WE LET YOU BORROW 10 BUCKS FOR A PACK OF SMOKES AND A BOTTLE OF NO-DOZ. HE'D BE LIKE,"BULLSHIT" THEN SNAP HIS HEAD FROM SIDE TO SIDE FOR LIKE A GOOD MINUTE, HE SCARED THE HELL OUT OF US!

THAT'S FREDDY. I HAD MOVED TO THE BAY AREA AND WAS DOING CONSTRUCTION BUT I WOULD COME HOME TO VISIT FROM TIME TO TIME

AND ONE WEEKEND THAT I WAS HOME I REMEMBER I WAS GETTING READY TO GO OVER THE BRIDGE FROM MARYSVILLE TO YUBA CITY. BEFORE I GOT ON THE BRIDGE THOUGH, OUT OF THE CORNER OF MY EYE I SAW THIS GUY IN "ALL CAMOFLAUGE" AND HE WAS "SNAPPING HIS NECK" FROM SIDE TO SIDE! I ALMOST WRECKED! HOLY SHIT,IT WAS FREDDY! SO I PULLED UP TO HIM, ROLLED DOWN THE WINDOW AND SAID, "WHAT THE HELL DO YOU THINK YOU ARE DOING SOLDIER?" HE JUST STARED AT ME LIKE HE WAS GOING TO KILL ME! DIDN'T SAY A WORD, JUST STARED ME DOWN! FINALLY I SAID, "FREDDY, IT'S MIKE!" MIKE KEARNS, JOE AND JACKS FRIEND! HE LOOKED PUZZLED THEN HE GOT THIS GREAT BIG SMILE ON HIS FACE AND SAID, "NNNOOOOO WAYYYYY!!" HEY MIKE, WHAT ARE YOU DOING BROTHER? I JUST SAID I WAS VISITING! HE THEN SAYS, "HEY MAN, I JUST LIVE OVER THE BRIDGE NOW, CAN YOU GIVE ME A RIDE?" HE THEN SAYS, "I REALLY GOTTA SHIT MIKE AND I DON'T THINK I CAN MAKE IT OVER THE BRIDGE WALKING!" I KNEW IF HE HAD TO STOP AND CRACK HIS LEGS IT WAS ALL OVER SO I TOLD HIM "SURE, JUMP IN!" WELL AS SOON AS WE START UP THE BRIDGE, I SMELL SHIT! AT FIRST I THINK HE MUST HAVE JUST FARTED, I GIVE HIM THE BENEFIT OF THE DOUBT. BUT AS WE GO A LITTLE FURTHER, THE SMELL GETS STRONGER. HE'S NOT SAYING A WORD! SO I'M LIKE, "FRED, YOU DOING OK OVER THERE?" HE JUST NODS AND SAYS NOTHING! BY THE TIME WE ARE OVER THE BRIDGE, I'M DRIVING WITH MY HEAD OUT OF THE WINDOW

ABOUT TO THROW UP! I YELL, OK FRED, WHERE DO I TURN? HE TELLS ME TO TAKE THE NEXT RIGHT AND WE FINALLY GET THERE! NOW HE CAN'T OPEN THE DOOR AND I'M JUST ABOUT READY TO VOMIT! HE FINALLY GETS THE DOOR OPEN AND I'M LIKE, "FREDDY, WHAT HAPPENED?" HE GOES, "WELL, I SHIT MYSELF BEFORE YOU PICKED ME UP AND I DIDN'T WANT TO TELL YOU BECAUSE I THOUGHT YOU WOULDN'T GIVE ME THE RIDE!" I'M LIKE "YOUR DAMN RIGHT I WOULDN'T HAVE!" HE JUST GOT A GRIN ON HIS FACE AND SAYS, "HEY YOU GOT ANY CIGS OR SOME CHANGE?" I'M THINKING ARE YOU KIDDING ME? I SAY, "NO DAMNIT, NOW GO CHANGE YOUR DAMN SHITTY PANTS!" HE'S LIKE, OK, WELL IT WAS NICE SEEING YOU MIKE! I'M LIKE "YEAH, GREAT!" I SPEED OFF AND THINK, "YEP, I GUESS PAYBACKS ARE A BITCH!"

"A THREE HOUR TOUR"

MY BROTHER "PAT" HAD A CANOE THAT MUST HAVE BEEN LIKE 20 FEET LONG. ONE DAY HE DECIDED TO CUT THE CANOE IN HALF AND HE FIBERGLASSED THE BACK END TO MAKE IT INTO A 10 FOOT BOAT. HE ALSO HAD A MOTOR THAT HE HOOKED UP TO THE BACK AND HE WOULD TAKE IT TO THE RIVER AND DRIVE IT AROUND, IT WAS A BLAST! HOWEVER, LIKE ANYTHING ELSE AS YOU GET OLDER, THINGS GET LESS FUN AND EVENTUALLY YOU QUIT DOING THE THINGS YOU USED TO. THIS IS WHERE "WE" COME IN!

DAN, JOE, CODY AND MYSELF DECIDED TO TAKE THE MOTOR OFF THE CANOE AND TAKE IT DOWN TO "REED'S CREEK!" THIS WAS A SMALL CREEK ABOUT 1 TO 1-1/2 MILES FROM OUR HOUSE, AND WE CARRIED IT ON OUR SHOULDERS.

EVERYBODY HAD BEEN BITCHIN BECAUSE THEY WERE TIRED OF CARRYING THIS THING UNTIL ALL OF A SUDDEN WE LOOKED OUT TO REED'S CREEK AND IT WAS "HUGE!" IT HAD RAINED FOR ABOUT 5 DAYS STRAIGHT BEFORE THIS AND THE CREEK HAD FLOODED AND IT WAS MOVING PRETTY GOOD. WHAT ONCE WAS THIS SMALL, NARROW CREEK HAD GREW BIG AS HELL BECAUSE OF THE CONSTANT RAIN!

WE SET SAIL (ALL 4 OF US) AND WE WERE SPLASHING A LITTLE BIT, WITH JOE KEPT SAYING,"QUIT SPLASHING ME I GOT MY NEW SCHOOL CLOTHES ON!" WE SAID,"JOE, WHY DID YOU WEAR YOUR GOOD CLOTHES TO THE CREEK YOU DUMBSHIT!" HE COULDN'T SAY ANYTHING!! BY THE WAY, IT WAS SUMMER VACATION AND WE HADN'T STARTED THE NEW SCHOOL YEAR YET!

WE STARTED GETTING BORED SO CODY AND I STARTED ROCKING THE BOAT FROM SIDE TO SIDE, ALMOST TIPPING IT OVER EACH TIME. I'M NOT SURE HOW DEEP IT WAS BUT WE WERE OUT IN THE MIDDLE! WE KEPT TIPPING IT WHEN ALL OF A SUDDEN IT CAPSIZED! WE STARTED SWIMMING. CODY AND I SWAM "WITH" THE CURRENT AND LET IT TAKE US TO A FENCE IN THE WATER WHILE DAN AND JOE SWAM "AGAINST" THE CURRENT. JOE WAS HAVING TROUBLE BUT I THINK HE CAUGHT ONTO SOMETHING AND WAS ABLE TO STAND UP WHILE DAN WAS YELLING FOR HELP BECAUSE HE WAS TOO

TIRED TO KEEP SWIMMING AGAINST THE STREAM. I WOULD DO ANYTHING FOR MY BROTHER (INCLUDING DYING FOR HIM) SO I SWAM OUT AGAINST THE CURRENT AND GRABBED DAN AND TOLD HIM TO JUST LET THE CURRENT TAKE HIM AND WHEN HE DID THIS HE WAS JUST FINE, HE WAS EVEN LAUGHING ABOUT IT WHEN IT WAS OVER! ONE PERSON WHO WASN'T LAUGHING WAS JOE!

I FORGOT TO SAY THAT WHEN JOE GOT UPSET AND YELLED HE HAD THIS HIGH, SQUEAKY TONE THAT WAS TOO FUNNY! SO HE STARTED YELLING,"WHY DID YOU TIP THE BOAT?" "YOU RUINED MY SCHOOL CLOTHES" AND YOU ARE GOING TO HAVE TO PAY FOR THEM! I GUESS THEY NEVER HEARD OF A WASHING MACHINE? IT WAS JUST DIRTY WATER, IT WASN'T PAINT!

WELL, THE BOAT SUNK, FOR GOOD! SO WE STARTED WALKING HOME AND CODY, DAN AND I WERE LAUGHING AND WONDERING HOW WE WERE GOING TO TELL PAT? JOE WAS JUST PISSED, TALKING TO HIMSELF (SOMETHING HE DID OFTEN) AND NOT JOINING IN WITH US! THE FUNNY THING WAS JOE WAS O.K. UNTIL WE CAME UP TO HIS HOUSE. AS SOON AS HE WALKED UP TO HIS DOOR HE STARTED CRYING REAL HARD AND SAYING "THEY TIPPED THE BOAT AND WRECKED MY SCHOOL CLOTHES" THEY DID IT ON PURPOSE! IT WAS MIKE AND CODY! CRYING SOME MORE

AND THEN JOYCE (JOE'S MOM) STARTED SCREAMING AND HITTING JOE! WE WERE GONE! WE FLEW DOWN THE ROAD BECAUSE WE DIDN'T WANT TO GET YELLED AT!

NEEDLESS TO SAY, WE WEREN'T ALLOWED OVER FOR AWHILE AND JOE COULDN'T PLAY WITH US FOR A WHILE, THE BIG PUSS!

WWF & FLATTS PIZZA

WHEN I WAS LIKE 10 YRS OLD AND DAN WAS LIKE 8, WE WERE INTO "BIG TIME WRESTLING" *BIGTIME!!* WE DID WATCH A LITTLE WCW AND ECW AND ANY OTHER WWW THAT WE COULD FIND BUT NOTHING COMPARED TO THE WWF!! THAT WAS OUR ALL TIME FAVORITE. THEY HAD WRESTLERS LIKE JYD (THE JUNKYARD DOG) THE BRITISH BULLDOGS, ANDRE THE GIANT, NICOLI VOLKOFF & THE IRAN SHIEK, KOKO B. WARE, RANDY "THE MACHO MAN" SAVAGE AND HIS MANAGER ELIZABETH (WHAT A BABE), BRETT THE HITMAN HART, SGT. SLAUGHTER AND LAST BUT NOT LEAST...HULK HOGAN!! EVERY FRIDAY NIGHT (UNTIL WE DISCOVERED GIRLS) WE FAITHFULLY WATCHED OUR WRESTLERS AND IT DIDN'T MATTER HOW MANY PEOPLE TOLD US IT WAS "FAKE" WE DIDN'T CARE! WE KNEW IT WAS REAL! I REMEMBER OUR

DAD TAKING US ON SATURDAYS TO "SCOTT'S BAKERY" IN MARYSVILLE TO GET A DONUT AND WHILE HE DRANK HIS COFFEE WE WOULD RUN NEXT DOOR TO THE LOCAL BOOKSTORE AND THEY HAD LIKE 3-5 WRESTLING MAGAZINES (AND ONCE AGAIN WE WERE BROKE) SO WE JUST STOOD THERE AND READ THE MAGAZINES WITH "DONUT FROSTING" GETTING ALL OVER THE PAGES, I KNOW THOSE MAGAZINES NEVER SOLD! ANYWAY, THESE

MAGAZINES WOULD GIVE YOU THE OUTCOME OF MATCHES ALL OVER THE WORLD FOR THE LAST MONTH AND THESE WERE GOOD FIGHTS TOO! USUALLY YOU KINDA KNEW WHO WAS GOING TO WIN OR SHOULD WIN (UNLESS RUSTY BROOKS WAS WRESTLING BECAUSE HE WAS A LEGEND WHO COULD DO SOME DAMAGE) AND SOMETIMES WE WOULD BE LIKE,"NO WAY!" THE OUTCOME OF THESE MATCHES WOULD MAKE YOU GO HMMM!

THE ONLY THING BETTER THAN WATCHING THESE FIGHTS ON FRIDAY NIGHT WAS TO HAVE PIZZA TO GO ALONG WITH IT! THE ONLY PROBLEM, YOUR RIGHT YOU GUSSED IT, NO MONEY. HOWEVER, THERE WAS ONE PLACE AND THEY OFFERED FREE DELIVERY AND THEIR PIZZA WAS THE CHEAPEST OF ANY PIZZA PLACE AROUND! MAYBE BECAUSE THE PIZZA FIT THE NAME "FLAT" AND IT PRETTY MUCH TASTED LIKE CARDBOARD! THE GOOD THING WAS WE GOT USED TO IT AND NOBODY EVER ASKED FOR MORE THAN (1) BITE! THE

HARDEST PART ABOUT GETTING THIS PIZZA WAS SCRAPING UP ENOUGH MONEY TO BUY IT AND I'M TALKING LIKE MAYBE $5.00 FOR A LARGE. WE WOULD SEARCH THE WASHER AND DRYER, UNDER THE WASHER AND DRYER, IN OUR DAD'S TRUCK,IN THE SOFA, IN MY MOM'S PURSE (WELL,I ALREADY GOT BUSTED FOR THAT IF YOU HAVEN'T ALREADY READ THAT STORY ☹) AND UNDER MY BROTHER'S BED. WHEN WE FINALLY GOT ENOUGH MONEY TO ORDER IT, WE HAD TO PAY IN A BUNCH OF PENNIES AND LOOSE CHANGE! WE PUT IT IN A ZIP LOCK BAG FOR THE PIZZA GUY! THE WORST PART...PAYING FOR IT. FOR ONE, WE ONLY HAD THE EXACT AMOUNT, FOR TWO, IT WAS ALMOST ALL IN CHANGE (SOMETIMES WE WOULD BE LUCKY AND HAVE A DOLLAR BILL)

AND THIRD, A TIP WAS TOTALLY OUT OF THE QUESTION! SO, HOW DID WE DECIDE WHO PAID FOR IT? WE DID "RO-SHAM-BO" OR ROCK, PAPER AND SCISSORS! I MUST SAY IT WAS PRETTY EVEN THE AMOUNT OF TIMES EACH ONE OF US HAD TO PAY BUT WHEN YOU WON, MY GOD THE SCREAM AND LAUGHTER WAS AS LOUD AS A GIRLS SLUMBER PARTY!! WE WOULD LAUGH AT THE OTHER ONE, TRY TO BRIBE HIM LIKE;"IF YOU DO IT THIS TIME THEN I WILL DO IT THE NEXT 3 TIMES" THE OTHER PERSON WAS LIKE "AWHH HELL NO!!" THAT NEVER HAPPENED IN OVER A YEAR, NOBODY WAS BUYING THAT!

THE PIZZA GUY OR GIRL (OW MAN IT WAS WORSE IF IT WAS A GIRL) WOULD COME AND I OR DAN WOULD STAND THEIR WHILE THEY COUNTED THE MONEY AND THEN WHEN THEY WERE DONE WE WOULD TAKE THE PIZZA AND ALWAYS SAY<"WE WILL GET YA NEXT TIME ON THE TIP." THEY WERE USUALLY PRETTY COOL ABOUT IT BUT YOU WOULD SOMETIMES GET THE SAME GUY WEEK AFTER WEEK AND HE KNEW WHEN WE OPENED THE DOOR THAT HE WAS GETTING "SHIT." HE WOULD SIGH, COUNT THE MONEY AND BEFORE WE COULD SAY IT, HE WOULD HAND OVER THE PIZZA AND SAY,"I KNOW, YOU'LL GET ME NEXT TIME!" NO WONDER THEY NEVER ASKED US IF WE WANTED CHEESE OR PEPPERS, "THE CHEAP BASTERDS!!"

BAD BOYS, BAD BOYS (COPS THEME SONG)

SO WE WERE AT SCHOOL ONE DAY JUST "KICKING IT" AND I'M SURE I WAS HAVING ANOTHER "YOUR MAMA'S SO FAT" DEBATE WITH SOME OTHER "WHITE TRASH BOYZ" WHEN ALL OF A SUDDEN CODY COMES UP AND SAYS HE HAS A "JOINT" (MARIJUANA CIGARETTE) AND DO I WANT IT? I SAID YES BUT I DON'T KNOW WHY BECAUSE OUR GROUP NEVER REALLY GOT INTO SMOKING WEED, WE JUST DRANK A LOT. I GUESS I FIGURED I COULD SELL IT TO SOME RETARDED CLASSMATE.

WE WERE ON THE BUS COMING TO SCHOOL (NOT A SMALL BUS EITHER...FULL SIZE BABY, ALL THE WAY) AND I WAS MESSING WITH THIS GUY NAMED "BILL" WHO WAS SLOW BUT SEEMED FASCINATED BY THE JOINT, WANTED TO HOLD IT WHICH I SAID, "NO MONEY NO FUNNY" SO HE DIDN'T GET TO HOLD IT AFTER ALL. ANYWAY I FORGOT ABOUT THE WHOLE THING UNTIL LUNCHTIME WHEN THE "DEAN" CAME OUTSIDE TO THE LUNCH AREA AND WANTED TO SEE ME IN HIS OFFICE. NOW "MR.X" AND I WERE PRETTY COOL, LAUGHING AND JOKING ALL THE TIME, EXCEPT THIS TIME. HE SEEMED PISSED. ALL OF A SUDDEN I KNEW THAT HE FOUND OUT ABOUT THE JOINT (WHICH I HAD IN MY WALLET)AND I WAS ABOUT TO BE BUSTED! AS WE WERE WALKING INTO THE OFFICE FROM OUTSIDE I TOOK MY WALLET OUT AND THREW IT ON THE GROUND, KNOWING MY FRIENDS WOULD PICK IT UP WHILE I WAS BEING QUESTIONED. GREAT PLAN EXCEPT AS WE WERE WALKING INSIDE MR.X LOOKED BACK, SAW MY WALLET AND PICKED IT UP. DAMN, I WAS SO BUSTED!!

WE GOT INTO HIS OFFICE AND HE TOLD ME THAT THIS BILL GUY TURNED ME IN FOR HAVING A JOINT, HE EVEN SAW THE JOINT AND NOW MR.X WANTED TO SEE IT. I TOLD HIM I DIDN'T HAVE IT, IT WAS ALL A JOKE, JUST PAPER WRAPPED UP TO LOOK LIKE IT! HE SAID, "BULLSHIT!" SAID I COULD EITHER SHOW HIM OR THE COPS COULD LOOK FOR

IT WHEN THEY CAME. WHOA, WAIT A MINUTE..COPS? HE SAID IF I SHOWED HIM NOW THEY WOULDN'T CALL THE COPS. I HAD THAT JOINT OUT OF MY WALLET SO FAST YOU WOULD HAVE THOUGHT I WAS A FAT KID AT AN ALL YOU CAN EAT BUFFET!!

MR.X DECIDED TO CALL MY DAD (A MATH TEACHER FOR 20+ YEARS AT A SCHOOL DOWN THE ROAD) AND HAVE HIM COME MEET WITH US AFTER SCHOOL, MAN WAS I DEAD!

BEFORE MY DAD GOT THERE, HERE COMES CODY, WHO GOT SENT TO THE "DEAN'S OFFICE" AS WELL FOR BEATING UP THAT BILL KID WHO TOLD ON ME FOR THE JOINT! WHAT A TRUE FRIEND! HE GOT A SLAP ON THE WRIST FROM MR.X, HE WANTED TO FRY "BIGGER FISH" I.E. ME!

MY DAD FINALY SHOWED UP...PISSED! I GOT (1)WEEK SUSPENSION AND MY DAD HAD PLENTY OF WORK FOR ME TO DO AROUND THE HOUSE DURING MY SUSPENSION! YOU THINK IT ENDS THERE, BUT YOU HAVE NO IDEA!

MY DAD _NEVER COMES HOME FROM TEACHING FOR LUNCH, EVER!_ SO WHAT HAPPENS NEXT? CODY SHOWS UP AT LUNCHTIME WITH A 12-PACK OF BEER! WE START DRINKING IT IN THE LIVING ROOM JUST WATCHING T.V. AND KICKING BACK, WHEN ALL OF A SUDDEN MY DAD PULLS UP! HE

NEVER COMES HOME FOR LUNCH! WE START RACING AROUND, PICKING UP BEER CANS, ETC. CODY RUNS OUT BACK TO HIDE AND IN WALKS MY DAD, NOT TOO HAPPY! HE SPOTS (1) BEER CAN (WE MISSED) SITTING ON THE FIREPLACE LEDGE AND SAYS,"PICK UP THE REST OF THE CANS, AND TELL YOUR FRIEND TO GET THE HELL OUT OF HERE. MY MOUTH JUST DROPPED OPEN. HOW DID HE KNOW? THEN HE SAYS,"YOU WANTED TO PLAY TODAY, GOOD. WELL TOMMORROW YOUR GONNA WORK." YOU BETTER GET SOME GOOD SLEEP TONIGHT! NO DOUBT, I HAD TO WORK MY ASS OFF! NOT ONLY THAT, BUT I ALSO LOST MY TICKETS TO GO SEE "BON JOVI" WHICH WOULD HAVE BEEN MY 1ST CONCERT EVER!

ALL THIS FOR A STUPID JOINT I DIDN'T EVEN SMOKE!! YEAH, MY DAD DIDN'T PLAY!!

"SCARY RIDE"

ONE CHRISTMAS SEASON I WORKED AS A CASHIER AT TARGET AND MET A LOT OF COOL PEOPLE. ONE NIGHT ONE OF THE CASHIERS WAS HAVING A PARTY AT HER HOUSE AND I DECIDED TO GO. HOWEVER, SINCE I KNEW I WAS GOING TO BE DRINKING AND DIDN'T WANT TO DRIVE I PARKED MY CAR AT THIS CO-WORKERS HOUSE WHO I WAS TRYING TO MESS WITH (SHE WAS LIKE 20 YEARS OLDER THAN ME...COUGAR) AND WE BOTH WENT TO THE PARTY IN HER CUSTOM VAN! WE HAD A GOOD TIME AND THEN DECIDED IT WAS TIME TO LEAVE (AFTER MIDNIGHT) SO WE DROVE HOME TO HER HOUSE, WELL...I FOUND OUT IT WAS HER AUNT AND UNCLES HOUSE AND HER SON WAS STAYING THEIR TOO. I DIDN'T WANT TO DRIVE SO I TOLD

HER I WOULD JUST SLEEP IN THE VAN UNTIL I WOKE UP AND DROVE HOME. SHE WAS O.K. WITH THAT AS LONG AS I WAS GONE BEFORE EVERYONE GOT UP. AFTER A LITTLE "GETTING DOWN WITH MY BAD SELF" SHE LEFT AND WENT INSIDE THE HOUSE WHERE IT WAS NICE AND TOASTY I'M SURE. IT WAS COLD AS COULD BE IN THAT VAN WITH NO BLANKETS OR ANYTHING! I THINK I SLEPT FOR ONLY ABOUT A HOUR OR TWO. FINALLY I DECIDED I HAD TO GO AND IT WAS LIKE 6:00 AM.

MY CAR WAS PARKED ON THE STREET AND I HAD ROLLED DOWN MY WINDOW ABOUT HALF WAY. I THOUGHT I WOULD START IT UP AND LET IT WARM UP BEFORE I GOT IN (BIG MISTAKE)! I REACH THROUGH THE WINDOW AND TURN THE KEY AND ALL OF A SUDDEN THE CAR STARTS UP AND STARTS DRIVING OFF, DRAGGING ME ALONG THE OUTSIDE WHILE MY JACKET IS CAUGHT IN THE WINDOW. I DIDN'T REALIZE THE CAR WAS "IN GEAR." I CANT REACH THE KEY TO TURN IT OFF, ALL I CAN DO IS STEER THE CAR! I'M SWERVING AROUND CARS, MISSING TRASH CANS UNTIL ALL OF A SUDDEN MY CAR IS COMING UP ON A HOUSE AND I HAVE A QUICK DECISION TO MAKE. I'M EITHER GOING TO RUN THROUGH THE FRONT YARD AND INTO SOMEONE'S LIVING ROOM OR SLAM INTO THE BACK OF A BIG VAN PARKED IN THE DRIVEWAY. I CHOOSE THE VAN AND ALL OF A SUDDEN YOU HEAR A HUGE CRASH AND MY CAR JUST KEEPS HITTING INTO THIS VAN! I'M FINALLY ABLE TO RIP MY JACKET

OUT OF THE WINDOW AND JUMP INTO THE CAR! REMEMBER, IT'S LIKE 6:00 AM AND QUIET AS CAN BE IN THIS LITTLE NEIGHBORHOOD BEFORE THIS. I BACK THE CAR OUT AND THE HOOD IS FOLDED IN HALF STICKING UP, WINSHIELD IS CRACKED, ETC. SINCE I HAVE BEEN DRINKING AND I'M PRETTY SURE I DIDN'T HAVE INSURANCE, I DECIDED TO "RUN."

PAT AND LIZ (MY BROTHER AND SISTER-IN-LAW) ONLY LIVED LIKE A MILE AWAY SO I HEADED OVER THERE, PRAYING A COP OR THE OWNERS OF THE VAN DIDN'T SEE ME OR CATCH UP TO ME...THEY DIDN'T ☺ I GOT OVER TO PAT AND LIZ'S AND WOKE THEM UP TO TELL THEM WHAT HAPPENED AND I'M SURE THEY WERE "NOT" SURPRISED WITH HOW I WAS LIVING MY LIFE AT THE TIME! THEY LET ME KEEP THE CAR THERE UNTIL I COULD FIGURE WHAT TO DO ABOUT IT. LATER ON THAT AFTERNOON, I TOOK MY MOM'S CAR AND DROVE BACK OVER TO THAT NEIGHBORHOOD TO SEE IF I COULD SEE ANYTHING OR GET A "VIBE" OF THINGS. AS I DROVE BY THE HOUSE AND VAN THAT I HIT, PEOPLE WERE OUTSIDE SITTING AROUND AND BOY WERE THEY STARING HARD AT ME! THAT OR I JUST "THOUGHT" THEY WERE? BOY WAS THE BACK OF THAT VAN JACKED UP! I JUST KEPT DRIVING LIKE I WAS LOOKING FOR A CERTAIN ADDRESS. SOON AS I ROUNDED THE CORNER, I MADE THE "SIGN OF THE CROSS" THANKED GOD FOR SAVING MY LIFE AND MADE A VOW TO NEVER DRI NK AGAIN FOR THE

REST OF MY LIFE! I'M SO GLAD WE HAVE A "FORGIVING GOD!" I THINK I WAS SPLITTING A 6-PACK LATER THAT EVENING? SO MUCH FOR THAT!

THE LADY NEVER MENTIONED IT TO ME SO I GUESS IT WAS A MYSTERY TO THE OWNERS OF THE VAN AND THE NEIGHBORHOOD! IT'S STILL TO THIS DAY THE SCARIEST RIDE I EVER TOOK!! I STILL GET CHILLS THINKING ABOUT IT!

."STOP, I CAUGHT YOU"

ONE DAY CODY AND I WERE HANGING OUT AT JOES HOUSE. WE WERE REALLY BORED. AS USUAL JOE HAD NOTHING GOOD TO EAT AND IF HE DID IT WAS PROBABLY ALREADY EXPIRED! WE WERE ALL WATCHING TV IN JOES MOM'S BACK BEDROOM. WE DECIDE TO LEAVE AND WE TOLD JOE WE WOULD CATCH HIM LATER! SO WE WALKED OUTSIDE. I TOLD CODY, "HEY LETS SNEAK BACK INSIDE JOES HOUSE AND WE WILL HIDE IN THE LIVING ROOM, THEN WHEN HE COMES OUT OF THE BACK BEDROOM WE WILL SCARE THE HELL OUT OF HIM! SO WE OPEN THE FRONT DOOR AS QUIETLY AS WE CAN, WE GO BEHIND THE COUCH AND THE LAZYBOY CHAIR. WE WAIT AND WAIT BUT HE DOESN'T COME OUT. I WHISPER TO CODY, "HEY, IM GONNA GO SNEAK A LOOK AND SEE IF JOES STILL LAYING ON THE BED!" QUIETLY I TIPTOE DOWN THE HALLWAY, GET TO THE ROOM AND I SLOWLY PEEK MY HEAD

INTO THE ROOM. THE TV IS STILL ON BUT JOE ISNT THERE. I LISTEN FOR A MINUTE AND I CAN HEAR SOME KIND OF TALKING COMING FROM THE BATHROOM THAT'S IN THIS ROOM. I QUIETLY CREEP UP TO THE BATHROOM DOOR TO SEE WHATS GOING ON. I SLOWLY LOOK INSIDE THE BATHROOM AND I JUST ABOUT LOST IT!! THERE INSIDE IS JOE, HIS PANTS DOWN TO HIS ANKLES. HE HAS HIS "LITTLE BUDDY" AND I DO MEAN "LITTLE" IN HIS HAND! THE TALKING I HAD HEARD WAS JOE, SAYING "COME ON BABY RISE, RISE!" OH C'MON BABY! ALL OF A SUDDEN I SCREAMED," STOP, I CAUGHT YOU!" YOU STOP RIGHT THERE! THEN I YELLED, "CODY,HURRY GET IN HERE RIGHT NOW! JOE HURRIES UP AND PULLS HIS PANTS UP. HE'S AS RED AS A TOMATO AND HAS A "DEER IN THE HEADLIGHTS" LOOK ON HIS FACE. CODY COMES IN AND SAYS, "WHATS GOING ON, WHAT HAPPENED?" I SAY TO JOE, "JUST TELL HIM WHAT YOU WERE DOING AND I PROMISE I WONT TELL ANYONE WHAT YOU WERE DOING!" JOE THINKS ABOUT IT FOR A MINUTE AND I REASSURE HIM THAT IT WON'T LEAVE THE BATHROOM! HE FINALLY DECIDES TO COME CLEAN AND SAYS TO CODY, "ALRIGHT, HE (BEING ME) CAUGHT ME JERKING OFF!" I WAS REALLY JUST PLAYING WITH MYSELF, I WAS BORED! THEN CODY LOOKS DOWN, SHAKES HIS HEAD IN A UNDERSTANDING WAY AND SAYS, "I HEAR YA DUDE, EVERYTIME I GET BORED THE FIRST THING I DO IS GO TO THE BATHROOM AND PLAY WITH MY JUNK!" WE BOTH BUST OUT

LAUGHING! THEN I SAY, "THANKS FOR ADMITTING WHAT HAPPENED" AND I WONT TELL ANYBODY! BY THE NEXT DAY AT SCHOOL I THINK I HAD ALREADY TOLD OVER 50 OF OUR FRIENDS! EVERYTIME THEY SAW JOE THAT DAY, THEY WOULD STOP AND GIVE HIM A STANDING OVATION! BOY HE WAS PISSED AT ME! I WAS SUCH A DICK! ☺

"SHOW AND TELL"

IT WAS 6TH GRADE YEAR AND THIS OPENED UP A WHOLE NEW WORLD OF OPPORTUNITY FOR GIRLS. YOU HAD KIDS COMING FROM THE THREE MAIN ELEMENTARY SCHOOLS OF OLIVEHURST, ELLA, AND OUR JOHNSON PARK TO FORM YUBA GARDENS. NOT THAT THE GIRLS WEREN'T OKAY FROM JOHNSON PARK BUT THE SELECTION HAD JUST MULTIPLIED. WELL, A PARTICULAR GIRL CAUGHT DAN'S EYE 6TH GRADE YEAR, HER NAME WAS KELLY. SHE WAS BEAUTIFUL. DAN THOUGHT SHE HAD IT ALL. THE NICE THING ABOUT KELLYY IS THAT SHE KNEW HOW TO KISS AND SHE WAS DIFFERENT FROM MOST GIRLS. SHE WANTED TO EXPERIMENT TOO. HEY, WHAT BOY WOULDN'T BE DOWN FOR THAT!

DAN AND KELLY HAD TALKED ALL SUMMER AND MADE A DEAL. THEY DECIDED TO MEET AT ARBOGA SCHOOL TO DO A LITTLE SHOW AND TELL. KELLY PROMISED TO LIFT UP HER SHIRT AS LONG AS DAN PULLED DOWN HIS PANTS. DAN RODE HIS BIKE TO THE SCHOOL ABOUT 2 MILES AWAY AND SURE ENOUGH KELLY SHOWED UP. THERE WAS A LITTLE BIT OF A TUG OF WAR ABOUT WHO WOULD GO FIRST AND THEY DECIDED TO GO ON THE COUNT OF 3. ONE, TWO, THREE AND SURE ENOUGH IT HAPPENED. IT WAS A DAY TO CELEBRATE.

JACK HAD RODE HIS BIKE THERE ALONG WITH DAN AS THERE HAD TO BE A WITNESS TO IT. ON TO THE CELEBRATION. JACK KNEW A BOY NAMED JIMMY WHO LIVED JUST DOWN THE STREET AND LIKED TO GET "HIGH". JIMMY HAD THE WORST JACKED UP TEETH YOU CAN EVER IMAGINE. DAN WAS NOT SOMEONE TO GET HIGH. HE WAS USUALLY THE GUY THAT SAID I'M GOOD WHEN THE JOINT WAS BEING PASSED AROUND , BUT THIS TIME CALLED FOR AN EXCEPTION. AFTER A COUPLE HITS, DAN PANICKED BECAUSE HIS BREATH NOW SMELLED AND HE DID NOT WANT TO GET IN TROUBLE AT HOME. WHAT WAS HE GOING TO DO? OUT OF DESPERATION, HE DECIDED TO BRUSH HIS TEETH. THE ONLY TOOTH BRUSH AVAILABLE WAS JIMMY'S. DID I MENTION JIMMY HAD THE WORST LOOKING TEETH AND GUMS IMAGINABLE. HOWEVER, GETTING IN TROUBLE AT HOME FOR SMOKING WAS NOT AN OPTION. NEEDLESS TO SAY, DAN MADE IT HOME, DIDN'T GET BUSTED, AND HE SAW HIS

FIRST BREASTS. LIFE WITH GIRLS HAD JUST BEGUN. BECAUSE DAN LIKES TO KEEP HIS "R" RATED STORIES TO HIMSELF TO PROTECT HIS FAMILY, MOST OF HIS ESCAPADES WITH GIRLD DID NOT MAKE THIS VERSION OF THE BOOK. , WE WILL LEAVE IT AT THAT.

"TEACHER OF THE YEAR"

WE HAD A TEACHER IN HIGHSCHOOL NAMED "MISS NIGHT" AND I NEVER SEEN ANYTHING LIKE IT. SOME TEACHERS ARE WEAK OR INTIMIDATED AND JUST CANT SEEM TO GET A HOLD OF THEIR STUDENTS. THE STUDENTS SEEM LIKE THEY JUST "TAKE OVER" AND PRETTY MUCH JUST RUN THE CLASS. BUT MISS NIGHT TOOK THE CAKE! SHE TAUGHT SEVERAL DIFFERENT CLASSES BUT MOSTLY SHE TAUGHT THE "LOWER LEARNING" STUDENTS AND THE "BONE HEAD CLASSES." HER CLASSROOM WAS ON THE 2ND FLOOR OF THE "C" BUILDING OVERLOOKING THE LIBRARY BELOW. SHE ALSO TAUGHT NEXT DOOR TO MR. WESSON'S CLASS. MR.WESSON WAS A BIG MAN. HE WAS LIKE 6'-5" AND HAD A REAL GRUFF VOICE. HE WASN'T MUCH FOR PLAYING AROUND! REAL SERIOUS! ANYWAY, BACK TO MISS NIGHT. I REMEMBER SITTING IN HER CLASS ONE DAY AND SHE WAS WRITING A POEM ON THE CHALKBOARD WHEN ALL OF A

SUDDEN YOU HEARD A LOUD "SMACK." SOMEBODY HAD THROWN THE BIGGEST, WETTEST "SPIT BALL" I HAVE EVER SEEN AT THE CHALKBOARD! NOW HER POEM HAD PRETTY MUCH BEEN WASHED AWAY, SHE HAD CAUGHT SOME "OVERSPRAY" FROM THE SPITWAD AND WAS WIPING HER FACE! THE STUDENTS WERE FALLING OUT IF THEIR SEATS LAUGHING AS SHE TRIED TO TAKE CONTROL OF THE SITUATION. SHE ASKED AROUND BUT OF COURSE NOBODY OWNED UP TO IT. SHE HAD A PRETTY GOOD IDEA OF WHO DID IT, BUT SHE COULDN'T BE A 100% SURE. ONE DAY WE WERE QUIETLY TAKING A TEST WHEN ALL OF A SUDDEN YOU HEARD A BIG "BANG" DOWNSTAIRS, RIGHT BELOW OUR CLASS. IT ECHOED THROUGH THE BUILDING. SLOWLY THINGS QUIETED DOWN AGAIN, HOWEVER ABOUT 5 MINUTES LATER IT HAPPENED AGAIN! THIS TIME A "TEACHERS AIDE" CAME STORMING UP TO OUR CLASSROOM CARRYING A HUGE TEXTBOOK! SHE TELLS MISS NIGHT THAT THE BOOK MISSED HITTING HER IN THE HEAD BY LIKE 5 FEET! SHE TOLD MISS NIGHT THAT SHE NEEDED TO CONTROL HER CLASS BETTER! UH OH, THAT REALLY ANGERED MISS NIGHT! SHE TOLD THE AIDE TO MIND HER OWN BUSINESS AND THAT MAYBE NEXT TIME IT WOINT MISS! I THOUGHT THE AIDE WAS GONNA SLAP MISS NIGHT RIGHT THERE! WELL MR. WESSON HEARD ALL THE COMOTION AND CAME OVER TO INTERVINE. HE ALSO TOLD MISS NIGHT THAT SHE NEEDED TO GET A HOLD OF HER CLASS! MISS NIGHT STARTS TO

TELL MR. WESSON OFF, BUT HE HAD ALREADY WALKED BACK TO HIS CLASS. ONE DAY MISS NIGHT CAME UP TO CODY AND SAID, "LISTEN CODY, YOU NEED TO QUIT TALKJING TO MIKE (ME) SO MUCH AND READ YOUR BOOK. WELL CODY THAN SAYS, "MISS NIGHT, I MEAN BETTY (THIS WAS MISS NIGHTS FIRST NAME) I NEED YOU TO STOP TELLING ME TO BE QUIET. MISS NIGHT SAYS, "CODY, DON'T CALL ME BY MY FIRST NAME THAT'S DISRESPECTFUL!" CODY THINKS FOR A MINUTE AND THEN SAYS, "I DON'T THINK YOU NEED TO CALL ME BY MY FIRST NAME, ITS DISRESPECTFUL. THE CLASS GOES CRAZY! MISS NIGHT THAN SAYS, "O.K. MR. LEWIS" NOW PLEASE BE QUIET. CODY SAYS, OK BETTY, THAT'S BETTER!" NOW HUSH!! ONE TIME CODY BROUGHT A CAMERA TO SCHOOL AND HE STARTED TAKING PICTURES OF MISS NIGHT. YELLING, READING, TEACHING. HE THEN LAYS ON THE FLOOR (LIKE A PHOTOGRAPHER TAKING BEACH SHOTS) AND SNAPS PICS LIKE THAT! MISS NIGHT IS NOW FURIOUS AND DEMANDS CODY GIVE HER THE CAMERA. CODY REFUSES AND TELLS MISS NIGHT TO PUSH OUT HER CHEST AND "WORK IT!" I STARTED CRYING I WAS LAUGHING SO HARD!! I FORGOT TO SAY MISS NIGHT WAS IN HER 60'S! EVENTUALLY CODY GOT MOVED TO A EVEN LOWER CLASS AND I GOT ON HER "GOOD SIDE." EARNING A SOLID C+.

WALL CHARGES

I'M NOT SURE WHO TOLD US ABOUT "WALL CHARGES" BUT THEY LEFT OUT THE PART ABOUT "YOU COULD POSSIBLY DIE!" WHAT A WALL CHARGE IS... A PERSON LEANS OVER WITH HIS HANDS ON HIS KNEES AND TAKES LIKE 8-10 HUGE BREATHES, HOLDING IN HIS LAST BREATHE HE RAISES UP, PUTS HIS BACK UP AGAINST A WALL AND LIKE 2 GUYS PRESS ON THE GUYS CHEST UNTIL HE GETS LIGHT HEADED AND FALLS TO THE GROUND. THE PERSON LIES ON THE GROUND FOR A FEW MINUTES UNTIL HE SLOWLY WAKES UP. THE PERSON USUALLY THINKS IT'S THE GREATEST THING! LIKE HAVING A HUGE "BUZZ" WITHOUT HAVING TO DRINK A TON OF ALCOHOL! HOWEVER, IT DOESN'T ALL GO THAT WAY! OUR FRIEND RONALD (WHO WEIGHED LIKE A BUCK 25, SOAKING WET) DID A WALL CHARGE ONE TIME AND AS THE GUYS WERE PUSHING ON HIS CHEST, HIS EYES ROLLED BACK IN

HIS HEAD, HE STARTED FLOPPING LIKE A FISH AND LOOKED LIKJE HE WAS HAVING A SEZUIRE. THIS LASTED ONLY A SHORT TIME BUT IT SURE SCARED THE HELL OUT OF US! FUNNY THING IS, EVEN AFTER WATCHING WHAT RONALD WENT THROUGH, THE REST OF THE GUYS STILL WANTED THEIR TURN! AMAZING!!

BOWS AND ARROWS

ALL OF US WERE REALLY INTO SPORTS. WE LIKED TO PLAY BASEBALL, BASKETBALL AND FOOTBALL! GOLF WAS CONSIDERED A "RICH MAN'S SPORT" AT THE TIME SO WE LEFT THAT ALONE. WE ALL PLAY NOW THOUGH AND IT'S GREAT! ONE SPORT WE NEVER GOT INTO WAS "SOCCER!" NOBODY REALLY PLAYED IT LIKE THEY DO NOW. DO YOU BLAME US? 1 GOAL SCORED EVERY 10 HOURS, NO THANKS!

BACK TO MY STORY. SO BEING INTO SPORTS WE NATURALLY LOOKED FORWARD TO P.E.!!

ONE YEAR WE GOT A GREAT SURPRISE. WE WERE GONNA START DOING ARCHERY OR AT LEAST PLAY GAME "SHOOTING ARROWS!" I STILL, TO THIS

DAY DON'T KNOW HOW THEY PUT MY BEST FRIEND CODY IN THE SAME P.E. CLASS?!! TROUBLE!!

ANYWAY, BEFORE YOU WALKED OUT TO THE FOOTBALL FIELD YOU WERE ISSUED A BOW AND (5) ARROWS. YOU GRABBED THEM YOURSELF OUT OF THE WOOD BOXES WHERE THEY WERE ALL NUMBERED! WHEN YOU GET OUT TO THE FOOTBALL FIELD YOU ALL SPREAD OUT "SIDE BY SIDE." THEN THERE WAS A ORANGE "CAUTION" CONE AT EACH END. WHEN THE COACH BLEW THE WHISTLE, YOU SHOT YOUR ARROW DOWN THE FIELD AND TRIED TO SEE WHO COULD GET THEIR ARROWS CLOSEST TO THE CONE! WELL THIS GAME WAS FUN FOR LIKE 10 MINUTES. CODY COMES UP WITH A GREAT IDEA! WE START CHECKING OUT OUR BOWS AND ARROWS AT THE BACK OF THE GROUP. WHEN WE NOTICE WHOS NOT THERE THAT DAY, WE TAKE ANOTHER STUDENTS ARROWS. THIS WAY ALL OUR ARROWS ARE BACK IN THE BOX AND ACCOUNTED FOR! NOW WE WILL BE SHOOTING SOMEONE ELSES!! THE PROBLEM WAS...CODY IS WAY TOO NUTS!! HE HAD ARROWS FLYING OVER CARS THAT WERE SPEEDING DOWN THE HIGHWAY ACROSS FROM THE FOOTBALL FIELD! OUR SCHOOL IS RIGHT NEXT DOOR TO A CEMETARY THAT HAD A GREAT POND WITH DUCKS AND A SMALL FOUNTAIN. SURE ENOUGH, YOU GUESSED IT! CODY WAS SHOOTING AT THE DUCKS WHILE HIDING FROM THE P.E. TEACHERS! EVERYDAY SHE WOULD GET BROKEN ARROWS RETURNED FROM THE GROUNDSKEEPER! HE WAS GETTING PISSED!!

NOT ONLY WAS THE CEMETARY CALLING ALMOST DAILY BUT RANDOM PEOPLE WHO WERE DRIVING O N THE FREEWAY WERE COMPLAINING HOW THEY ALMOST WRECKED FROM BEING "UNDER ATTACK!" THE SCHOOL COULDN'T FIGURE OUT WHO WAS DOING THIS BECAUSE EVERYTIME THEY CHECKED THE NUMBERS ON THE ARROWS THEY WERE THAT OF A STUDENT WHO WAS OUT SICK THAT DAY OR WASN'T IN CLASS. SO THEY HAD NO OTHER CHOICE BUT TO "SCRAP THE PROGRAM." THANKS A LOT CODY!!

"WHO FARTED"

THERE WAS A GIRL WHO WAS A FEW YEARS OLDER THAN ME THAT I GUESS YOU WOULD SAY WE WERE "FRIENDS WITH BENEFITS." IF THAT IS THE WAY KIDS TODAY REFER TO IT? "BECKY BROTHERS" WAS A GIRL WHO WAS A FEW GRADES AHEAD OF US BUT MOST OF HER FRIENDS WERE MY AGE SO WE HUNG OUT OFF AND ON A LOT. IT SEEMED LIKE WHEN ONE OF US WASN'T DATING SOMEONE ELSE, WE WOULD GET TOGETHER AND MESS AROUND. WELL, ONE FRIDAY NIGHT I GOT A CALL FROM "BECKY" WANTING TO SEE WHAT I WAS DOING THAT NIGHT. SINCE I REALLY DIDN'T HAVE ANY PLANS EXCEPT TO HANG OUT WITH CODY, THE JOHNSON BROTHERS AND OUR FRIEND DARRYL, I TOLD HER THAT WE WERE JUST GOING TO GET SOME BEER AND MESS AROUND. THE COOL THING WAS "BECKY" HAD A FAKE I.D. AND COULD BUY ALCOHOL SO THIS WORKED OUT GREAT! WE DIDN'T HAVE TO FIND ANYONE TO BUY! SHE SAID SHE WAS GOING TO BE "PARTYING" AT HER FRIEND "SUSAN'S" HOUSE AND WE COULD COME OVER THERE! SCORE!! THE ONLY BAD THING WAS THAT BECKY PROMISED SUSAN THEY COULD GO TO THIS

DANCE CLUB IN TOWN CALLED "GOO-GOO'S" WHERE SUSAN WAS SUPPOSED TO MEET THIS AIR FORCE GUY SHE MET AT THE MALL. SINCE MY FRIENDS AND I COULDN'T GET IN, SUSAN AGREED TO LET US STAY AT HER HOUSE UNTIL THEY GOT BACK. REALLY? HOW DUMB WAS THAT!! THE GUYS WERE ALL FOR THIS! I TOLD THEM TO FOLLOW ME ON MY MOTORCYCLE BECAUSE I PLANNED ON GOING "EXTRA INNINGS" WITH BECKY AND WOULD PROBABLY STAY WAY LATER THAN THEM. ANYWAY, WE GOT OVER TO SUSAN'S HOUSE AND WERE ALL DRINKING AND HAVING FUN. ONE COOL THING FOR ME WAS WHENEVER BECKY GOT "BUZZED" SHE LIKED TO KISS AND MAKE OUT!! I WAS GOOD WITH THAT AS WELL! I THINK CODY GOT A LITTLE JEALOUS THOUGH BECAUSE HE WOULD NOT QUIT HITTING ON SUSAN! SHE DIDN'T WANT ANYTHING TO DO WITH CODY, AT LEAST NOT YET. SHE THOUGHT SHE WAS GOING TO HOOK UP WITH THIS "AIRMAN" AT THE CLUB. WELL, WE DRANK FOR A FEW HOURS UNTIL FINALLY THE GIRLS DECIDED TO GO DANCING FOR A LITTLE BIT. BECKY DID NOT WANT TO GO AT THIS POINT, WE WERE "IN A GROOVE!" BUT SHE PROMISED HER FRIEND SO SHE HAD TO GO. SHE MADE ME PROMISE TO BE HERE WHEN SHE GOT BACK AND THAT SHE WOULD "TOTALLY MAKE IT UP TO ME" AS SOON AS SHE GOT BACK. WHAT COULD I SAY, NO? SO I PROMISED HER AND THEY LEFT. WE PLAYED QUARTERS FOR AWHILE, WATCHED PART OF A GIANTS GAME THAT WAS BEING REPLAYED AND JACK & DARRYL BROKE INTO SUSAN'S PARENTS "LOCKED BAR" AND WERE TAKING TURNS PLAYING "BARTENDER." THE DRINKS TASTED LIKE SHIT! THEY WOULD BE 3 QUARTERS ALCOHOL AND MAYBE A SPLASH OF SODA! THEY WERE STRONG! I FORGOT TO MENTION SUSAN'S PARENTS WERE GONE OUT OF

TOWN FOR THE WEEKEND. THIS IS THE ONLY REASON WE WERE THERE!

TIME PASSED AND THE BOYS WERE GETTING TIRED AND READY TO GO. JUST ABOUT THAT TIME, SUSAN AND BECKY GOT HOME. I GUESS SUSAN GOT "STOOD UP" AS THE AIRMAN NEVER SHOWED UP! TOO BAD! WHAT DOES CODY DO? TRIES TO ACT CONCERNED AND COMFORT SUSAN. IT LOOKED LIKE IT WAS WORKING TOO! THEY WENT INTO SUSAN'S ROOM AND WERE IN THERE FOR A LITTLE WHILE UNTIL ALL OF A SUDDEN CODY COMES OUT, HE'S PISSED! HE'S GOT VOMIT ON HIS SHIRT AND HE'S HOLDING HIS NOSE. I GUESS THEY WERE MAKING OUT WHEN SUSAN GOT SICK AND THREW UP ON CODY, THE BED, EVERYWHERE. HE WAS GONE! HE TOLD THE GUYS, "LET'S GO" AS WE WERE ALL JUST BUSTING UP!! SO THEY LEFT AND BECKY HELPED SUSAN CLEAN UP AND GET INTO BED. I WAS PRETTY DRUNK AT THIS POINT AND WORSE THAN THAT...I HAD GAS BAD! I KEPT FARTING AND FANNING IT AWAY FROM ME! IT WAS FUNNY WHEN THE GUYS WERE HERE, I COULD BLAME IT ON JOE OR CODY! BUT NOW IT WAS JUST ME. I TRIED TO HOLD IT INSIDE BUT THEN MY STOMACH WOULD CRAMP UP. I TRIED TO WALK AROUND AND NOT STAY IN THE SAME SPOT BUT THESE STUNK BAD! I NEVER SHOULD HAVE HAD BURRITOS FOR DINNER! ANYWAY...BECKY CALLS ME INTO SUSAN'S ROOM (SUSAN STAYED IN HER PARENTS ROOM THIS NIGHT) AND SHE IS READY TO "FULFILL HER PROMISE." SO WE ARE LAYING ON THE BED, MAKING OUT. HOWEVER, I KEEP HAVING TO FART! SO I STOP KISSING AND SIT UP FOR A MINUTE. BECKY ASKS IF EVERYTHING IS OK AND I SAY "OH YEAH, I'M JUST STRETCHING!"I GOT A CRAMP! THE GOOD THING IS BECKY IS PRETTY DRUNK BY THIS TIME AND IS HAVING A HARD TIME STAYING AWAKE!

ANY OTHER TIME I WOULD BE MAD, BUT TONIGHT IT WAS GOOD BECAUSE THE GAS WAS BAD! AS I'M SITTING THERE, LAYING NEXT TO BECKY, I HAVE TO FART. SO I PROCEED TO FART, ONLY THIS TIME IT WAS NO FART!! I THINK I JUST "SHIT MY PANTS!" SO I'M LAYING THERE, MY LEGS ARE UNDER HERS AND I CAN'T GET OUT! MY EYES ARE AS BIG AS FRISBEES AND I'M THINKING "OH SHIT!" LITERALLY! WHAT AM I GONNA DO?? I WAIT TO SEE IF THAT "FART SMELL" GOES AWAY BUT IT DOESN'T. YEP, I HAD AN ACCIDENT! LUCKILY, BECKY IS "OUT" AT THIS POINT. SO I LIFT HER LEGS OFF MINE AND SHE WAKES UP FOR A SECOND, MUMBLES SOMETHING AND GOES BACK TO SLEEP! CLOSE CALL! SO I CAREFULLY SLIDE OFF THE BED TRYING NOT TO WAKE HER! IT'S DARK BUT I SWEAR I SEE "WET SPOTS" ON THE SHEETS THAT "I MADE!" DAMN! THANK GOD I WASN'T WEARING SHORTS!!

I TIPTOE OUT OF THE ROOM, OUT OF THE HOUSE AND GET ON MY MOTORCYCLE AND I'M GONE. I GET HOME AND EVERYONE IS ASLEEP. I GET IN THE SHOWER AND CLEAN UP. WHAT A NIGHT! THE NEXT DAY I GET A CALL FROM BECKY ASKING ME WHAT HAPPENED LAST NIGHT! I'M THINKING, "OH SHIT" I'M BUSTED! SHE SAID SHE COULDN'T REMEMBER ANYTHING ABOUT LAST NIGHT. THE LAST THING SHE REMEMBERED WAS MAKING OUT WITH ME IN SUSANS ROOM. SHE DIDN'T MENTION ANY "POOPY SHEETS" SO I DIDN'T EITHER! I JUST TOLD HER THAT WE WERE LYING DOWN, GETTING READY TO DO WHAT PEOPLE DO AND THAT SHE PASSED OUT! ALWAYS THE GENTLEMAN, NOT WANTING TO TAKE ADVANTAGE OF SOMEONE WHO WAS DRUNK...I JUST TUCKED HER INTO BED, KISSED HER GOODNIGHT AND WENT HOME. SHE THOUGHT I WAS THE GREATEST GUY FOR HAVING SO MUCH RESPECT FOR HER AND FOR

HANDLING THE SITUATION LIKE I DID, THAT ABOUT A WEEK LATER WE "HANDLED BUSINESS" AND I MADE SURE I SHOWED UP ON A "EMPTY STOMACH!" ☺

"HOW WAS CHURCH"

GROWING UP IN A CATHOLIC HOUSEHOLD MEANT GOING TO SUNDAY MASS EVERY WEEK! THE CATHOLIC RELIGION ISN'T LIKE OTHER RELIGIONS LIKE "CHRISTIAN CHURCHES" OR "BORN AGAIN"ONES. IN CHRISTIAN CHURCHES IT'S BIG TO INVITE NEWCOMERS TO CHURCH, OR TO BRING YOUR FRIENDS TO SERVICES. SOME EVEN HAVE GREAT BANDS THAT ATTRACT NEW, YOUNG PEOPLE TO IT. WHILE THAT SEEMS GREAT, THE CATHOLIC CHURCH IS JUST THE OPPOSITE. NO ROCK BANDS INSTEAD YOU HAVE 80 YEAR OLD SISTER MARY MARGRET "TAKING YOUR REQUESTS!" OK, NO REQUESTS BUT THE SAME SONGS OVER AND OVER!! ANOTHER DIFFERENCE BETWEEN CATHOLIC MASS AND A CHRISTIAN SERVICE IS THE "WORKOUT!" AT A CATHOLIC MASS, ITS 45 MINUTES OF STANDING, SITTING, KNEELING, ONE LAP INSIDE THE BUILDING (FOR COMMUNION) AS OPPOSED TO A CHRISTIAN SERVICE OF MAYBE STANDING FOR A MINUTE IN THE BEGINNING THEN SITTIN FOR THE REST.

WELL, SINCE OUR PARENTS DEMANDED WE GO EVERY SUNDAY, MY BROTHERS CAME UP WITH A PLAN TON GET AROUND THIS. USUALLY MY PARENTS WOULKD GO TO 10:30AM MASS, SO MY BROTHERS AND I WOULD GO TO THE 9:00AM MASS. THE PROBLEM WAS THAT OUR PARENTS ALWAYS THOUGHT THEY COULD "BUST US" FOR NOT GOING BY ASKING WHO THE PRIEST WAS AND/OR WHAT HIS SERMON WAS ABOUT. SO, TO BEAT THEM AT THIS "GAME" MY BROTHER DAN AND I WOULD FLIP A COIN AND WHO EVER LOST HAD TO CLIMB THE STEPS AND PEEK THROUGH THE DOORS TO SEE WHO THE PRIEST WAS. THEN WE WOULD GRAB A BULLETIN SO WE COULD SEE WHAT THE TOPIC THAT WEEK WAS ABOUT! THEN WE HAD A HOUR TO KILL. WE WOULD GO AND DRIVE THE "BACKROADS" MAYBE DRIVE TO CAMP FAR WEST? ROADS WHERE NOBODY HARDLY WAS SO THAT MY BROTHERS COULD SMOKE A JOINT IN PEACE. MY BROTHER DAN AND I WOULD JUST SIT BACK, RELAX AND GET A "CONTACT HIGH" FROM ALL THE SMOKE IN THE CAR! I KNOW WE GOT A LITTLE "STONED" BECAUSE AFTER ABOUT 10 MINUTES OF THEM SMOKING, WE COULDNT STOP SMILING AND LAUGHING. I KNOW THIS MADE MY BROTHERS NERVOUS BECAUSE THEY DIDN'T WANT MY PARENTS TO FIND OUT! THE GOOD THING THOUGH WAS THAT BY THE TIME WE GOT HOME, MY PARENTS WOULD BE GONE TO CHURCH AND WE WOULD BE OFF PLAYING WHEN THEY GOT HOME! FUN TIMES FOR SURE! THE ONLY THING THAT CHANGED ALL THIS WAS "BREAKFAST!" IF WE WENT TO CHURCH WITH MY BROTHERS THEN WE DIDN'T GET TO EAT! THERE MONEY WAS FOR WEED! HOWEVER, IF WE WENT TO CHURCH WITH MOM AND DAD, THEN WE DID GET BREAKFAST. THERE WERE 3 OPTIONS MY DAD HAD. 1. WE JUST GO HOME AND MOM MAKES BREAKFAST OR 2. WE GET TO GO TO JACK IN THE BOX (OUR

FAVORITE) OR 3. WE GET TO GO TO " EAT AND RUN DONUTS!" OUR BEHAVIOR IN MASS DETERMINED WHERE WE WOULD GO. WE WERE SO DUMB SOMETIMES. WE WOULD START GIGGLING ABOUT SOMETHING AND MY DAD WOULD GIVE US THE EVIL EYE. THIS USUALLY WORKED WITH MY BROTHER AND I BUT SOMETIMES WE JUST COULDN'T STOP. YOU KNOW WHEN SOMETHING IS JUST SO DAMN FUNNY THAT YOU CAN'T HELP BUT KEEP LAUGHING, THAT WAS LIKE THIS! WE WOULD BITE ON OUR FINGERS, STOP LOOKING AT EACH OTHER, THINK ABOUT SOMETHING REALLY BAD, ANYTHING! BUT NOTHING WORKED! HOPEFULLY ALL THE LAUGHING HAPPENED IN THE BEGINNING AND MY DAD WOULD FORGET ABOUT IT BY THE END OF MASS! THIS WAY WE WOULD STILL HAVE A CHANCE AT "JACK IN THE BOX!"

AS WE WOULD DRIVE OFF FROM CHURCH, MY BROTHER AND I WOULD "CRUNCH" DOWN IN OUR SEATS AND WE HAD THE TURNS DOWN IN OUR HEAD! IF WE WENT A CERTAIN DISTANCE AND THEN TURNED RIGHT, WE WERE GOING TO DONUTS! IF WE STAYED STRAIGHT AND WENT A LITTLE FARTHER...IT WAS "JACK!" BUT IF WE DID A DREADED LEFT TURN, THEN WE WERE ON OUR WAY HOME FOR "BACON AND EGGS!" DAMN! WE WOULD "SIGH" REALLY BIG AND GO "UMMMMMHHH" BASICALLY LETTING OUR PARENTS KNOW WE WERE VERRY DISAPPOINTED! THIS WOULD GO ON LONG ENOUGH FOR ONE OF THEM TO POINT OUT HOW BAD WE WERE IN CHURCH AND HOW WE EMBARRASED THEM! HOW WE DIDN'T DESERVE BREAKFAST AT ALL! IT'S TRUE AND EVERYTHING BUT WHEN YOUR YOUNG LIKE THAT YOU DON'T KNOW HOW TO "PLAY THE GAME" YET! LIFE GOES ON, WITH OR WITHOUT A "BREAKFAST JACK!"

"CAN I TAKE YOUR ORDER"

WHEN I TURNED 16 I GOT MY FIRST REAL "PAYING" JOB, WE WILL CALL THE PLACE "BURRITO GONG" BUT IM SURE YOU CAN FIGURE OUT ITS REAL NAME. MY FRIEND "OTIS" GOT ME THE JOB BECAUSE HE WORKED THERE AND THEY REALLY LIKED HIM! SHIT, WAIT TILL THEY GET A HOLD OF ME! THE SMELL WAS GREAT! IN THE BEGINNING THE FOOD WAS GREAT TOO! WHEN YOU WORKED, YOU COULD EAT FOR FREE! I ADMIT AFTER ABOUT A MONTH, THAT GOT OLD. EXCEPT TO MY BROTHER DAN. HE COULD AND WOULD EAT IT EVERYTIME I BROUGHT FOOD HOME! I'LL GET TO THAT IN A MINUTE. AT FIRST THE JOB WAS COOL. THEN SINCE I WAS NEW (AND YOUNG) THEY GAVE ME ALL THE SHIT JOBS. CLEAN THIS, WASH THIS, GO HELP UP FRONT! ONE OF THE WORST JOBS WAS MAKING BEANS! YOU HAD TO MAKE BIG BIG POTS OF BEANS! IT WAS HARD WORK AND YOU HAD TO STAY WITH

IT OR THEY WOULD BURN AND I WOULD GET MY ASS CHEWED! HAPPENED QUITE A BIT. NOT JUST FOR BURNT BEANS THOUGH! LOOK, I WAS THE "FUNNY FAT KID" I HAD MY REPUTATION TO UPHOLD! WHEN I WOULD GET REALLY PISSED, I WOULD "EXPERIMENT" WITH DIFFERENT INGREDIENTS. I WOUKD BE OFF BY THE TIME THEY USED MY BEANS ANYWAY! EXCEPT I WAS TOO DUMB TO REALIZE I HAD INITIALED THE POTS WITH MY INITIALS!! OH WELL, I MADE THE GROUND BEEF A LITTLE HOTTER A FEW TIMES WITH SOME CHILI SAUCE AND STUFF! SOME CUSTOMERS ENJOYED IT HOT, WHILE OTHERS DIDN'T SEE THE HUMOR IN IT! THEY DIDN'T ENJOY "RUNNING FOR THE BORDER" OR OUR RESTROOM!! SORRY!

AS I SAID MY BROTHER DAN JUST LOVED THIS FOOD AND THEY LET US TAKE HOME ANY "MESS UPS" THAT WE MADE WRONG. WE WOULD JUST PUT THEM IN THE WALK-IN AND TAKE THEM HOME WHEN WE WERE OFF! I USED TO MAKE SO MANY "MISTAKES" ON PURPOSE SO I WOULD HAVE A TON OF FOOD TO BRING DAN! SOMETIMES WHEN IT WAS SLOW, I WOULD TELL THEM I WAS MAKING MYSELF SOMETHING FOR LATER. THEY WOULKD ALL BE OUT BACK SMOKING ANYWAY. DAN LOVED THIS ITEM WE WILL CALL A "BITCHARITO." IT WAS LIKE A ENCHILADA. I WOULD MAKE IT "GRANDE" FOR SURE! I WOULD PUT LIKE A POUND OF BEANS, 2 POUNDS GROUND BEEF, ½ POUND OF CHEESES AND

A SEPERATE CUP OF SAUCE HE COULD PUT ON LATER. I SWEAR THIS THING WAS AMAZING! IT HAD TO WEIGH 4-5 POUNDS EASY! A LOT OF TIMES I WOULKD BRING HOME ONE OF THOSE, A COUPLE BURRITOS, A FEW TACOS, ETC. I DON'T KNOW WHERE DAN PUT IT BUT HE ATE ALL OF IT! EVERYTIME I BROUGHT IT HOME!! WELL, AFTER AWHILE AND A FEW "WRITE- UPS" (THEY FAILED TO SEE THE HUMOR IN MY ACTIONS) IT WAS TIME FOR ME TO FIND OTHER WORK! LUCKY FOR ME,I HAD ANOTHER FRIEND (LETS CALL HER "KEISHA")WHO WAS AN ASSISTANT MANAGER AT ANOTHER FAST FOOD PLACE IN TOWN AND WAS ABLE TO GET ME HIRED AT "RALPH'S SENIOR" AGAIN....FIGURE IT OUT!

THIS PLACE WAS A LOT DIFFERENT! I LIKED IT A LOT BETTER! THE FOOD WAS REALLY GOOD TOO! NO FREE FOOD HERE BUT YOU GOT 50% OFF WHEN YOU WORKED! WELL, THERE WAS WAYS AROUND THAT TOO! I WILL TELL YOU IN A MINUTE. THEY ALSO HAD PRETTY GIRLS WORKING THERE, THAT WAS NICE! IN FACT, THE MANAGER (LETS CALL HER "CANDY") HAD A THING FOR YOUNG MEN IN MY AGE RANGE. SHE WAS MARRIED BUT IT WAS LIKE A OPEN MARRIAGE BECAUSE HE DID HIS OWN THING AND SHE DID HER OWN THING. I THINK "THEY" STOPPED DOING THINGS WITH THEMSELVES BUT HE WAS ALLOWED TO "CRASH" AT HER PLACE WHEN HE WAS IN TOWN. HE WAS A TRUCK DRIVER AND WAS GONE MOST THE TIME.

HEY, SHE WAS LONELY AND SHE WAS MY BOSS! WANTING TO BE A "TEAM PLAYER" I FELT LIKE IT WAS MY DUTY TO "PLAY BALL!" ☺ MORE ON THAT IN A MINUTE!

THEY SEEMED TO LIKE ME A LOT HERE SO I WAS ABLE TO PUT IN A GOOD WORD FOR MY BEST FRIEND CODY AND HE GOT HIRED AS WELL! WE WORKED A LOT OF THE SAME SHIFTS BECAUSE OF SCHOOL AND IT WAS FUN AS HELL! WE USED TO DO ALL KINDS OF STUFF! ONE THING WAS WE WERE ALWAYS PRETTY MUCH BROKE. SO WE WOULD HOOK EACH OTHER UP ORDERING AND MAKING FOOD! FOR INSTANCE. I WOULD TAKE CODYS ORDER. HE WOULD ORDER THE SMALLEST, CHEAPEST BURGER WE HAD. AT THE TIME, THIS "KIDS BURGER" WAS LIKE 80 CENTS. THEN HE WOULD ORDER A SMALL FRY. THIS WAS LIKE 60 CENTS. HE GOT HIS "HALF OFF" DISCOUNT SINCE HE WAS WORKING SO IT CAME UP TO LIKE .75 CENTS WITH TAX. THEN I WOULD GO IN THE BACK AND MAKE HIS FOOD. WE HAD TO DO THIS WHEN IT WAS SLOW WHEN HARDLY NOBODY WAS WORKING AND THE MANAGER WAS IN HER OFFICE! EMPLOYEES HAD TO EAT IN THE BACK BREAKROOM, SO IT WASN'T NOTICEABLE ANYWAY. THE THING IS, SOMEHOW I READ THE TICKET WRONG,BECAUSE INSTEAD OF MAKING A KIDS BURGER I ENDED UP MAKING A BURGER WITH 3-1/2 POUND PATTIES, ALL THE VEGGIES, CHEESE AND MUSTARD YOU COUKLD FIT. THEN INSTEAD OF A SMALL FRY, FOR SOME

REASON I MADE CODY A HUGE "BASKET" OF FRIES! IT FILLED A TRAY! HE DID GET A SMALL SODA THOUGH, BECAUSE SODA WAS FREE! TRY TO PICTURE ALL THIS FOOD! NO WONDER WE WERE GETTING FAT!!

WELL, BACK TO "CANDY" ONE FRIDAY NIGHT A CO-WORKER OF OURS (A GUY OUR AGE WHO WAS IN A SERIOUS RELATIONSHIP) HAD A PARTY AT HIS PLACE. WE WERE OVER THERE DRINKING (CANDY BOUGHT A PONY KEG FOR THE PARTY)HAVING A GREAT TIME UNTIL THE GUYS "JEALOUS" GIRLFRIEND COMES OVER AND STARTS A BUNCH OF SHIT WHICH ENDED THE PARTY EARLY! WELL, CANDY WAS BUZZING JUST LIKE ALL OF US AND STILL WANTED TO PARTY! WE DECIDED TO GO "SKINNY DIPPING" IN BEAR RIVER (JUST OUTSIDE OF WHEATLAND) BUT WE NEEDED SOME DRY CLOTHES FOR WHEN WE GOT OUT. CODYS PARENTS WERE HOME SO WE COULDNT GO THERE BUT MY PARENTS HAPPENED TO BE OUT OF TOWN SO WE WENT TO MY HOUSE. I COULDNT BELIEVE IT, HERE WE ARE PARTYING WITH OUR BOSS! CODY AND I WERE DETERMINED TO "GET RAISES" TOGETHER THAT NIGHT!! SO WE GO BACK TO MY HOUSE AND CODY IS IN THE BATHROOM. CANDY IS SITTING ON MY BED AND I HAVE MY BACK TO HER AS I WAS GETTING HER SOME "SWEATS" TO WEAR. ALL OF A SUDDEN, I TURN AROUND AND CANDY IS TOTALLY NAKED JUST SMILING FROM EAR TO EAR. MY MOUTH DROPPED TO THE FLOOR! HERE I'M 16 YEARS

OLD AND THIS IS A WOMAN! AN ATTRACTIVE WOMAN. SO I GET UP AND GO SIT BY HER ON THE BED. SHES NOT COVERING UP OR NOTHING! I GIVE HER THE SWEATS AND SHE THANKS ME WITH A BIG KISS. I'M THINKING TO MYSELF, "OH MAN THIS IS GONNA HAPPEN!!" ALL OF A SUDDEN CODY BUSTS IN THE ROOM AND IS LIKE HURRY UP GUYS, UNTIL HE SEES CANDY(NAKED) AND STOPS TALKING. HES JUST LOOKING HER UP AND DOWN AND HIS MOUTH HIT THE FLOOR! CANDY JUST LAUGHS, PUTS HER SWEATS ON AND GOES, "LAST ONE TO THE CAR GETS NOTHING!" WE START RUNNING AFTER HER AND IM YELLING "SHOTGUN, SHOTGUN!" CODYS LIKE DAMN! THAT'S MESSED UP!

SO WE DRIVE THE 7 MILES OR SO TO BEAR RIVER (WE ARE DRINKING FROM THE KEG THAT'S IN CANDYS HATCHBACK ALL THE WAY THERE) AND WE WALK DOWN TO THE WATER. IT'S A NICE NIGHT AND THE WATER WAS ACTUALLY NOT TO COLD. WE ALL GET UNDRESSED, CODY AND I WITH OUR BACKS TO CANDY. WHILE SHE JUST RIPS THEM OFF AND WALKS IN. SHES PRETTY RIPPED BY NOW! WE ARE ALL BUZZING GOOD! SO WE ARE SWIMMING AROUND AND CODY SWIMS OVER TO CANDY AND THEY KINDA WRESTLE FOR A MINUTE. I THINK HE STEALS A KISS BUT SHE SWIMS AWAY. HE JUST LOOKS AT ME AND SMILES, THEN HE POINTS OVER TO HER AND MOTIONS FOR ME TO GO OVER TO CANDY. WELL, FINALLY I SWIM OVER BY HERE AND SHE PULLS ME INTO HER ARMS. THEN SHE LAYS

THIS HUGE KISS ON ME, MY MOUTH NOW FILLED WITH THIS HUGE TONGUE GOING A MILE A MINUTE! IM THINKING DAMN! SLOW DOWN! FINALLY WE SEPARATE BUT BEFORE WE DO SHE SAYS,"YOU BOYS THINK YOU CAN HANDLE THIS?" IM LIKE, OH HELL YEAH! SHE SAYS O.K. LETS GO BACK TO YOUR HOUSE AND TAKE CARE OF BUSINESS!! SO I GO TELL CODY AND HE JUST ABOUT FLIPS OUT! WE ARE LIKE 2 FAT KIDS IN A CANDY STORE WITH TONS OF MONEY!! WE CANNOT BELIEVE THIS IS GONNA HAPPEN!! SO, LIKE I SAID CANDY WAS BUZZING HARD AND SHE WAS GOING PRETTY FAST. I TOLD HER SHE BETTER SLOW DOWN THROUGH WHEATLAND BECAUSE THEY ARE NOTORIOUS FOR GIVING SPEEDING TICKETS. WELL, SURE ENOUGH AS SOON AS WE GET THROUGH WHEATLAND, HERE COMES THE LIGHTS...WE ARE GETTING PULLED OVER! CANDY IS BUZZING AND SAYING, "DON'T WORRY GUYS I GOT THIS" AND IM THINKING WE HAVE A OPEN KEG, 2 16 YEAR OLDS WHO HAVE BEEN DRINKING, NOT GOOD! WELL THEY MAKE CANDY DO A DUI TEST AND OF COURSE SHE FAILS. LUCKILY THEY DIDN'T SEE THE KEG IN THE BACK! BUT THEY THROW CANDY IN THE BACK OF THEIR CAR AND TELL US THEY ARE TAKING HER TO YUBA COUNTY (MARYSVILLE) TO GET BOOKED FOR DUI! THEY TELL US THAT WE ARE FREE TO GO, GET OUT OF THERE. SO WE SAY, LOOK WE LIVE IN THE NEXT TOWN, ON YOUR WAY TO YUBA COUNTY, CAN YOU GIVE US A RIDE? THE COP IS LIKE, IF I GIVE YOU GUYS A RIDE ITS TO YUBA COUNTY AND YOU

WILL GET ARRESTED AS WELL, STILL WANT A RIDE? WE ARE LIKE NO SIR, WE WILL WALK. SO THEY LOCK UP CANDYS CAR AND PULL AWAY. WE ARE LIKE GREAT. WE LEFT OUR SHIRTS, WE LEFT JACKETS. ALL WE HAD WAS WET SHORTS AND WET SHOES ON! WE STARTED WALKING AND IT WAS PITCH BLACK, ITS AFTER MIDNIGHT AND IM SUPPOSED TO WORK AT LIKE 6AM. IM LIKE IM CALLING IN SICK! NOBODY WOULD PICK US UP! DON'T BLAME THEM, I WOULDN'T EITHER! THE DAMN NOISES AT NIGHT ARE SCARYING THE HELL OUT OF US. TALK ABOUT SPEED WALKING. WE SET A RECORD THAT NIGHT. WE FINALLY GET HOME AND I CALL WORK. I TELL THE ASST. MANAGER THAT IM NOT COMING IN. SHES LIKE WE GOT NOBODY ELSE THAT CAN WORK, YOU GOTTA COME IN. IM LIKE WHAT ABOUT CODY (THAT'S MESSED UP HUH ☺) AND SHES LIKE NO WAY, HE CANT WORK BREAKFAST! I FINALLY SAID LOOK, I WAS WITH CANDY (THE MANAGER) TONIGHT AND SHE GOT IN TROUBLE, WE HAD TO WALK A LONG WAY AND IM NOT COMING IN! SHES LIKE, WELL, I DON'T KNOW ABOUT ANY OF THAT BUT YOU BETTER COME IN THIS MORNING OR YOU ARE IN BIG TROUBLE! I SAID WE SHALL SEE AND HUNGUP! I WENT TO BED AND SLEPT FOR HOURS. I CALLED CANDY WHEN I GOT UP AND SHE JUST SAID SHE WAS IN THE DRUNK TANK FOR LIKE 4 HOURS. SHE GOT HER CAR BACK THAT GOT TOWED AND WAS BASICALLY JUST EMBARRASED. I TOLD HER ABOUT NOT WORKING AND SHE SAID YEAH, SHE HAD ALREADY GOT A CALL ABOUT IT AND FOR ME

TO NOT WORRY ABOUT IT! I WAS LIKE COOL! SHE THEN SAID, LETS NOT MENTION THIS TO NOBODY, TELL CODY NOT TO EITHER. SHE THEN SAYS, SHE WANTS TO FINISH WHAT SHE STARTED BUT WITH JUST ME NOT CODY! I SAID OK ANYTIME. WORK WAS KINDA WEIRD AFTER THAT FOR AWHILE BUT EVENTUALLY THINGS WENT BACK TO NORMAL AND ABOUT A MONTH LATER....WE DID FINISH WHAT WE STARTED!! BEST 2 MINUTES OF MY LIFE!! HA HA!!

WILD TURKEY 101

CODY LEWIS AND I PLAYED ON A CO-ED SOFTBALL TEAM IN THE MARYSVILLE REC. LEAGUE. WE PLAYED ON THE "BURRITO GONG" TEAM (I STAYED FRIENDS WITH SOME OF THE GUYS I WORKED WITH AFTER I GOT FIRED) AND IT WAS PRETTY FUN. HAVING NOT BEING THAT GREAT IN SPORTS, I COULD HIT A SOFTBALL AND I PLAYED A MEAN FIRST BASE! CODY PLAYED SHORTSTOP I BELIEVE AND HE WAS OK BUT HE "THOUGHT" HE WAS BETTER THAN HE ACTUALLY WAS! IT WAS FUN BECAUSE WE COULD (AND DID) WEAR OUR FLOWER SHORTS AND WILD SOCKS TO THE GAMES! THE CROWD LOVED IT, OUR TEAM MEMBERS MAYBE NOT SO MUCH! ANYWAY, AFTER 1 PARTICULAR GAME WE MET UP WITH DAN KEARNS, RONALD LOVE AND A

FEW OTHERS. THEY WANTED TO GO MESS AROUND AT THE YUBA SUTTER FAIR. CODY AND I WERE ALL FOR IT BUT WE SAID LETS "CATCH A BUZZ" BEFORE WE GO. EVERYONE WAS DOWN FOR THAT BUT WE DIDN'T HAVE A LOT OF MONEY AND WE WOULD HAVE TO FIND SOMEONE TO "BUY" FOR US. CODY WAS LIKE SCREW THIS, LETS GO TO "VACATION MARKET" IN OLIVEHURST AND I WILL "BORROW" A BOTTLE OF SOMETHING. WE WERE LIKE O.K. MAKE SURE YOU GET SOMETHING STRONG. SO 5 MINUTES LATER, CODY COMES OUT WITH A HUGE BOTTLE OF WILD TURKEY 101 (101 PROOF=STRONG) AND WE WERE EXCITED! WE ALL WENT TO CODYS AND WE CHANGED REAL QUICK THAN WE WERE OFF TO THE FAIR. DRINKING AND DRIVING (STUPID AS IT IS) WAS MORE ACCEPTABLE BACK THEN AND ALOT OF PEOPLE (INCLUDING US) DID THIS. SO WE WERE PASSING THE TURKEY AROUND, ALL MAKING FACES AS WE DRANK IT! THIS STUFF WAS GROSS AND STRONG! IT WOULD PUT HAIR ON YOUR CHEST FOR SURE! WELL WE GOT TO THE FAIRGROUNDS AND I WAS LIKE, "I'M NOT EVEN BUZZING YET!" THEN RONALD SAYS, "THIS STUFF IS CALLED CREEPER LIQUOR BECAUSE ALL OF A SUDDEN IT WILL CREEP UP ON YOU AND YOU WILL BE ALL SHIT FACED!" WE ALL LAUGHED AND I SAID, "OH REALLY GENUIS, BEEN DRINKING ALONG TIME HUH?" EVRYONE LAUGHS AGAIN AND RONALD JUST SAYS "WHATEVER, FUCK YOU!" SO I TELL THEM TO GO AND I'M GONNA FINISH IT THEN I WILL CATCH UP TO THEM INSIDE THE FAIR. THEY WERE LIKE

"WHATEVER" AND LEFT. WE WERE PARKED ABOUT A $\frac{1}{4}$ MILE FROM THE ENTRANCE AND IT TOOK ME LIKE 20 MINUTES OR SO TO FINISH THE BOTTLE. THE THING IS, I WAS DRUNK AS HELL NOW AND I DIDN'T EVEN KNOW IT! SO I TAKE OFF FOR THE FAIR. THE NEXT 20 MINUTES OR SO ARE PRETTY HAZY AND I DON'T REMEMBER MUCH BUT THE LAST THING I REMEMBER IS WALKING IN THE FAIRGROUNDS (STUMBLING) LOOKING FOR A BATHROOM! I REALLY REALLY HAD TO PISS! NEXT THING I KNOW, 2 POLICE OFFICERS (ONE ON EACH SIDE OF ME) ARE THERE ASKING ME HOW IM DOING. I SAY, "I'M NOT FEELING TOO GOOD, I THINK I'M GONNA THROW UP!" BY THIS TIME THE ALCOHOL HAS CAUGHT UP TO ME AND OH YEAH, I FORGOT TO MENTION WE DRANK THIS ON A EMPTY STOMACH EXCEPT FOR THE BAG OF FUNYUNS WE PASSED AROUND! DAMN FUNYUNS ARE GOOD TO EAT WHEN YOUR DRINKING! ANYWAY, THE POLICE MEN TAKE ME OVER TO A FENCE AWAY FROM EVERYONE AND I START PUKING MY BRAINS OUT! I EITHER "PISSED MYSELF" OR DIDN'T HAVE TO GO ANYMORE, I FORGET. WHEN I GET DONE, THEY PUT ME IN HANDCUFFS AND SAY I'M GONNA BE ARRESTED FOR TACKLING A OLDER LADY AND TRYING TO STEAL HER PURSE! I'M LIKE "WHAT?" YEAH, I'M SURPRISED AS MUCH AS YOU ARE! I DID NOT DO THIS! I KNOW IM DRUNK BUT IM ALWAYS A MELLOW DRUNK JUST HAPPY, NEVER VIOLENT! FOR SOME REASON, INSTEAD OF TAKING ME TO JAIL THEY CALLED MY PARENTS! CANT BELIEVE I

REMEMBERED THE NUMBER! ANYWAY, MY MOM AND DAD GET THERE AND MY DAD STARTS TALKING TO ONE OF THE COPS. LUCKILY HE WAS A FORMER STUDENT OF MY DADS (MY DAD WAS HIS MATH TEACHER IN 8TH GRADE) AND MY MOM IS OVER TALKING, PLEADING WITH THIS LITTLE OLD FILIPINO LADY (SUPPOSEDLY THE ONE I TACKLED AND TRIED TO TAKE HER PURSE)TO DROP THE CHARGES! THE LADY FELT SORRY FOR ME BUT HER HUSBAND WAS PISSED! MY MOM BEGGED THIS LADY, SAYING "PLEASE LET MY SON GO, HES A GOOD KID AND HE LEAVES FOR THE NAVY IN 2 WEEKS. IF HE GETS ARRESTED THEN HE CANT GO IN THE NAVY!" FINALLY THE LADY DECIDED TO DROP THE CHARGES AND I WAS FREE TO GO WITH MY PARENTS. THIS WAS NOT A FUN RIDE HOME! MY DAD WAS YELLING, MY MOM WAS CRYING AND ALL I COULD SAY WAS THAT THIS WAS ALL BULLSHIT! I DID NOT DO THIS! WE DRANK LIQUOR YES, BUT THATS IT! WELL INSTEAD OF RESTRICTION, THEY DECIDED I HAD TO GET OUT OF THE AREA UNTIL I LEAVE FOR BOOTCAMP WHICH WAS 2 WEEKS AWAY. SO I MOVED IN WITH MY OLDEST BROTHER KEVIN, WHO LIVED IN SAN JOSE. I STAYED WITH HIM UNTIL LIKE 5 DAYS BEFORE I LEFT FOR THE NAVY! I DRANK THERE TOO! BUT WAIT, THERES MORE! NOW WE FIND OUT WHAT REALLY HAPPENED THAT NIGHT! SO IT SEEMS THAT THE GUYS GOT WORRIED ABOUT ME BEING ALONE DRINKING THE WILD TURKEY SO THEY SENT RONALD BACK TO GET ME AND TAKE ME TO WHERE THEY WERE. RONALD

EXPLAINED ALL THIS TO MY PARENTS THE NEXT DAY! ANYWAY, AS RONALD CAME BACK TO GET ME, HE SAW ME ALL STAGGERING ON MY WAY TO THE ENTRANCE. THEN HE SAW ME GO UP TO THIS LADY, PICK HER UP AND HUG HER FROM BEHIND AND SAY, "DAN, I LOVE YOU MAN!" THEN I ACCIDENTLY LOST MY FOOTING AND FELL BACK WITH THIS LADY IN MY ARMS. WE HIT THE GROUND, SHE LANDED ON TOP OF ME AND DID NOT GET HURT THEN I MUST HAVE REALIZED IT WASN'T DAN AND STARTED OFF FOR THE ENTRANCE AGAIN. BTW, RONALD SAID I ABSOLUTELY DID NOT TRY TO TAKE HER PURSE! THAT WAS HER HUSBAND LYING! I KNEW I DIDN'T! ANYWAY, I GUESS WHEN I GOT TO THE ENTRANCE, I JUST WALKED ON THROUGH, DIDN'T BUY A TICKET, DIDN'T LISTEN TO THE PEOPLE, JUST KEPT ON WALKING. RONALD WAS LAUGHING BUT SHAKING HIS HEAD AT THIS POINT! ABOUT THIS TIME, I GOT REPORTED AND THAT'S WHEN THE POLICE CAME UP ON ME AND ASKED HOW I WAS DOING! THAT'S THE STORY! I GUESS THE MORAL TO THE STORY IS....DON'T DRINK ON A EMPTY STOMACH, DON'T DRINK WILD TURKEY 101 AND IF YOU DO, LIKE RONALD SAYS, " THIS STUFF IS CALLED CREEPER LIQUOR BECAUSE ALL OF A SUDDEN IT WILL CREEP UP ON YOU AND YOU WILL BE SHIT-FACED!" MAN...NO KIDDING!! SOME PEOPLE NEVER LEARN!!

WANNA DANCE BIG BOY

WE HAD A FRIEND BACK IN HIGH SCHOOL, WE WILL CALL HIM "TAD." ANYWAY, TAD WAS A SENIOR AND WE WERE FRESHMAN. HE TOOK A LIKING TO US RIGHT AWAY. WE THOUGHT HE WAS PRETTY COOL TOO! HE HUNG AROUND MOSTLY JUST GIRLS BUT HE THOUGHT WE WERE FUNNY SO HE LIKED US TOO! TAD WAS PRETTY FEMININE BUT WE NEVER THOUGH TO MUCH ABOUT IT BECAUSE LIKE I SAID, HE WAS ALWAYS AROUND GIRLS AND STUFF. WELL ONE FRIDAY WE WERE TALKING TO TAD AND HE WAS ASKING WHAT WE WERE GOING TO DO THAT NIGHT. WE WERE LIKE, "PROBABLY NOTHING BECAUSE THERE IS NOTHING TO DO IN THIS TOWN!" SO TAD SAYS, "HOW WOULD YOU GUYS LIKE TO GET OUT OF TOWN AND GO TO THIS AWESOME DANCE CLUB IN SACRAMENTO?" WE WERE LIKE OH HELL YEAH BUT WE CANT GET IN, WE ARE UNDERAGE. TAD IS LIKE, ":DON'T WORRY ABOUT IT, YOU GUYS WILL GET IN, THEY DON'T CARD!" HELL YEAH WE WANNA GO! HOWS THE MUSIC? YOU SURE THEY WILL DANCE WITH US? HE REASSURED US THAT IT WAS ALL GOOD! HE HAD A MINI VAN AND HE SAID HE WOUKLD PICK US UP AT

CODYS HOUSE AT NLIKE 8:30PM. WE ALL WENT HOME, WE WERE GETTING READY, CALLING EACH OTHER BACK AND FORTH LIKE A BUNCH OF BITCHES, IT WAS TOO FUNNY! WE MET AT CODYS HOUSE AT LIKE 7:30PM WE WERE EXCITED. IT SEEMED LIKE FOREVER BUT TAD FINALLY GOT THERE AND WE LOADED IN! IT WAS ME, DAN, JOE AND JACK JOHNSON AND CODY! I THINK TAD HAD A JOINT. WE DIDN'T REALLY SMOKE BUT TAD KEPT PRESSURING US TO "GET HIGH" SO WE DID.I DON'T KNOW WHAT KIND WE WERE SMOKING BUT MAN IT WAS POTENT! WE WERE ALL LAUGHING AND GETTING STUPID ON THE WAY. WE FINALLY GOT TO THE CLUB. THE FUNNY THING ABOUT IT WAS THAT IT WAS WAY OUT BY ITSELF AND WE HAD TO PARK PRETTY FAR AWAY! ANYWAY, WE GET UP TO THE PLACE AND IT HAD LIKE CHRISTMAS LIGHTS, STROBE LIGHTS, SMOKE, ETC. TAD WAS RIGHT, NOBODY CARDED US, SO THAT WAS COOL! ONCE WE GOT INSIDE, TAD SAID JUST LOOK AROUND AND HE WOULD BE RIGHT BACK. REMEMBER NOW WE ARE KINDA STONED! SO WE ARE STANDING ON A WALL FACING THE DANCE FLOOR. PEOPLE ARE DANCING BUT IT LOOKS LIKE ITS GIRLS WITH GIRLS AND GUYS WITH GUYS! AT FIRST WE THOUGHT, "OH, ITS LIKE SCHOOL DANCES WHERE THE GIRLS ARE SHY AT FIRST, THE GUYS DON'T REALLY WANT TO DANCE SO THE GIRLS DANCE TOGETHER WITH EACH OTHER FOR AWHILE. THAT WAS COOL BUT THEN WE ARE LIKE, "ARENT THOSE GUYS DANCING TOGETHER?" THEY WERE. SICK! WE WERE LIKE "THAT'S GROSS!" I THINK CODY ASKED A GIRL TO DANCE AND SHE TURNED HIM DOWN! THEN JACK ASKED ANOTHER GIRL AND SHE WAS LIKE "I DON'T THINK SO LITTLE BOY!" HE WAS PISSED! I WAS LIKE, "I GOTTA USE THE BATHROOM" AND CODY WAS LIKE ME TOO! SOI WE GO TO THE BATHROOM AND WE GO TO PISS IN THE URNUAL AND ONE GUY SHAKES THE

OTHER GUY OFF AS HE FINISHES PISSING! THEN WE LOOK TO THE RIGHT AND THE 2 GUYS NEXT TO US ARE ALL STARING AT OUR JUNK! WE TURN AWAY AND CODY ALMOST PISSES ON MY LEG! AND WHERE THE HELL IS TAD? WE LEAVE THE BATHROOM AND KINDA ALL HUDDLE UP. WE TELL THE OTHERS ABOUT WHAT HAPPENED IN THE BATHROOM AND WE FIGURE OUT IT'S A GAY CLUB! DUH! I KNOW WE ARE SLOW HUH? ANYWAY, WE DECIDE TO HAVE SOME FUN! THE ONE THING GOING FOR IT WAS IT DID HAVE GREAT MUSIC PLAYING! SO WE DECIDE TO ACT GAY FOR AWHILE AND PLAY IT OFF! SO I GET CODY AND LEAD HIM TO THE DANCE FLOOR. DAN TAKES JACK OUT THERE TOO! JOE IS JUST WATCHING. ITS A FAST SONG AND WE JUST START TEARING IT UP! WE ARE BOUNCING AROUND, WE GOT ON THIS LIKE SMALL TABLE AND START DANCING, CODY SLAPS MY ASS AND I RETURN THE FAVOR! JOE COMES OUT AND WE START DANCING 3 WAY! AND…WHERE THE HELL IS TAD?? WE DO THIS FOR LIKE 2 SONGS, GUYS ARE STARTING TO NOTICE US NOW AND WE ARE ABOUT TO LOSE IT! THEN A SLOW SONG COMES ON! WE GRAB EACH OTHER AND START TO DANCE FOR ABOUT 30 SECONDS WHEN ALL OF A SUDDEN I HEAR CODY YELL, "YOU BUNCH OF FAGS!" JOE YELLS, "FIND THE SAUSAGE!" AND WE ARE OUTTA THERE!! WE START RUNNING AS FAST AS WE CAN TOWARDS THE VAN, WHEN ALL OF A SUDDEN WALKING TOWARDS US FROM THE VAN IS TAD AND SOME TOTALLY FEMINE GUY! "HE'S LIKE WHERE YOU GUYS GOING?" WE GO "FUCK YOU TAD, TAKING US TO A GAY BAR!" YOU'RE A DICK!! TAD JUST STARTS LAUGHING AND RUNNING TO THE VAN WITH US! WE PILE IN AND GET ON THE WAY BACK TO MARYSVILLE. NOW TAD SWEARS THAT THIS WAS ALL A BIG JOKE! THAT HE JUST WANTED TO PLAY A TRICK ON US! HE SAID SOMEBODY PULLED THE SAME JOKE ON HIM AND HE THOUGHT IT WOULD BE

FUNNY! WELL THE FUNNY THING WAS TAD COULDN'T TELL US WHERE HE DISAPPERED TO! ALL HE SAID WAS THAT WHEN WE GOT HERE HE HAD TO GO TO THE BATHROOM. WHEN HE WAS IN THE BATHROOM HE NOTICED HE DIDN'T HAVE THE CAR KEYS. SO HE WAS LOOKING AROUND AND THE GUY HE WAS WITH STARTED HELPING HIM LOOK. THEY BACK TRACKED ALL THE WAY TO THE VAN. HE SAID THEY FOUND THE KEYS BY THE VAN. WE WERE LIKE, "THIS TOOK THE WHOLE TIME WE WERE HERE?" HE SAID YEP! HE DIDN'T WANT TO DISCUSS IT! OH WE BELIEVE THEY WENT BACK TO THE VAN ALRIGHT. WE JUST THINK THEY WERE "BOBBING FOR APPLES" OR SOMETHING!!

WE DIDN'T REALLY HANG OUT WITH TAD AFTER THAT AND HE SEEMED JUST FINE WITH THAT! HE GRADUATED AND THEN I THINK HE MOVED AWAY. SOMEBODY SAID THEY HEARD SAN FRANCISCO BUT IM NOT SURE?

MAY I HAVE THIS DANCE

      I REMEMBER ONE TIME OUR FRESHMAN YEAR WE DECIDED TO GO TO ONE OF THE SCHOOL DANCES! WELL OF COURSE WE THOUGHT WE HAD TO GET A LITTLE "BUZZ" BEFORE WE WENT. I'M NOT SURE IF I MENTIONED THIS IN ANOTHER STORY FROM THIS BOOK OR NOT AND I'M TOO LAZY TO GO BACK AND LOOK SO I WILL JUST TELL YOU ABOUT IT AGAIN. IF YOU ALREADY READ IT THAN I APOLIGIZE! HERE GOES. COMING FROM A FAMILY OF (6) BOYS AND LIVING IN A SMALL 3 BEDROOM 1 BATH HOUSE, THINGS WERE CRAMPED! EACH ROOM WAS SMALL TO. 2 OF THESE BEDROOMS WOULD BE LIKE YOUR 1 BEDROOM IM SURE! YOU HAD ROOM FOR 2 BEDS, A DRESSER, CLOSET AND THAT'S IT! WELL, IF YOU DO THE MATH, THAT'S NOT ENOUGH ROOMS! 1 FOR MOM AND DAD, 1 MORE FOR 2 BOYS AND THE LAST ONE FOR 2 BOYS. THAT LEAVES 2 BOYS RIGHT? MY DAD WAS A MATH TEACHER, I GOT

THAT BASIC ADDITION SUBTRACTION ALL FIGURED OUT!! SO, MY DAD BUILT A ROOM IN THE GARAGE WHERE THE 2 OLDEST COULD STAY! NO BATHROOM, BUT IF YOU JUST HAD TO GO PEE, IT WAS OUT THE BACK DOOR INTO THE BACKYARD AND IN THE BUSH!! NOW THIS ROOM WAS PRIMARILY USED FOR ROLLING JOINTS, SMOKING THEM AND THEN SITTING BACK TO ENJOY LED ZEPPLIN. IT WAS A PRETTY COOL ROOM BUT I REMEMBER MORE THAN ONCE MY DAD GOING OUT THERE, FINDING THE GREEN STUFF AND FLUSHING IT ! MY BROTHERS WERE NOT HAPPY! ANYWAY, I'M WAY OFF THE STORY! LET ME GET BACK TO THE DANCE! BY THIS TIME, THE OLDER BROTHERS HAD ALL MOVED OUT AND DAN AND I HAD OUR CHOICE OF SLEEPING IN THE HOUSE OR OUT IN THE "GARAGE ROOM." WE KINDA LIKED THE WARMTH OF THE HOUSE SO WE STAYED IN THERE. HOWEVER, WE WOULKD HANG OUT IN THE GARAGE ROOM FROM TIME TO TIME. LISTENING TO MUSIC, WATCHING TV, ETC. WELL ON THIS PARTICULAR NIGHT, CODY CAME OVER BEFORE THE DANCE AND HE HAD JUST MADE A STOP AT THE STORE WHERE HE "BORROWED" 2 BOTTLES OF JACK DANIEL'S WHISKEY! GOD I HATED THE SMELL, THE TASTE, ALL OF IT! BUT IT DID GET US BUZZED! MISSION ACCOMPLISHED! SO WE START WALKING TO THE HIGH SCHOOL TO THE DANCE AND WE ARE DISCUSSING HOW WE NEED TO ACT COOL SO WE CAN GET IN! THEY HAD THIS SECURITY LADY, MARGE. WE CALLED HER "SARGE" AND SHE WAS

TOUGH! SHE WAS A GREAT LADY BUT HARD AS HELL TO GET ANYTHING PAST HER! SHES AT THE ENTRANCE DOOR WATCHING EVERYONE LKE A HAWK AND ITS COMING UP TO OUR TURN TO PAY. SO WE ARE GOOFING OFF BUT I THOUGHT WE WERE DOING PRETTY GOOD. WE GO TO PAY AND SARGE SAYS, "STEP OVER HERE GENTLEMEN!" SHIT! WE ARE GONNA GET CAUGHT! SHE CALLS FOR THE DEAN TO COME OVER AND WE ALL WALK TO THE FRONT OFFICE. I TELL CODY, PLAY IT COOL DUDE. IF THEY TRY TO SMELL YOUR BREATH, THEN JUST BREATHE IN! WE ARE ACTING LIKE "WHATS GOING ON?" THIS IS STUPID! THEY ASK US IF WE HAVE BEEN DRINKING AND WE ARE LIKE NO! WE DON'T DRINK! WHAY ARE YOU HASSLING US? THEN THE DEAN HAS US BREATHE ON HIM! WE DID WHAT WE SAID AND JUST SUCKED IN! HE WAS SO LAME! HE DIDN'T EVEN CATCH ON! ALL OF A SUDDEN "SARGE" GETS A CALL ON HER RADIO ABOUT A FIGHT GOING ON AND SHE TAKES OFF TO GO HANDLE THAT! THE DEAN SAYS, "YOU HAVENT HAD ANYTHING TO DRINK?" WE ARE LIKE NO WAY MAN, WE DON'T EVEN LIKE ALCOHOL! SO HE SAYS O.K. AND LETS US GO BACK TO THE DANCE! WOW! TALK ABOUT CLOSE CALLS! I THOUGHT WE WERE BUSTED FOR SURE!! SO WE ARE HAVING A GOOD TIME, FEELING A LITTLE BUZZED BUT GOOD! I'M TEARING UP THE DANCE FLOOR LIKE A YOUNG JOHN TRAVOLTA AND THEN THE SONG ENDS. I GO SIT IN A BOOTH OPPOSITE OF CODY AND HIS GIRLFRIEND. NOW "BETTY" USED CODY HARD! AND CODY WAS "WHIPPED!" I GUESS

BECAUSE BETTY WOULKD HAVE SEX WITH HIM WHEN EVER SHE WANTED SOMETHING! TOTAL USER! I DIDN'T TRUST HER FOR NOTHING! SHE WAS A TEASE TO ME! I REMEMBER SITTING THERE AND YOU KNOW HOW GIRLS ALWAYS HAD THEIR SHOES OFF AT DANCES, WELL SHE STARTS PUTTING HER FOOT IN MY LAP. NEXT THING I KNOW SHES RUBBING MY BALLS WITH HER FOOT! SHES JUST LOOKING AWAY OR TALKING TO CODY BUT JUST WORKING ON THE "FAMILY JEWELS!" I WAS GONNA SAY SOMETHING TOO BUT I WANTED TO MAKE SURE THIS WAS REALLY HAPPENING! OK IT WAS, BUT INSTEAD OF SAYING ANYTHING I JUST GOT UP, "ADJUSTED" AND WENT TO DANCE. WELL I'M OUT THERE DANCING AND THE NEXT THING I KNOW, CODY IS OUT THERE DANCING (HE NEVER DANCES) AND THEY ARE MAKING LIKE A CIRCLE AROUND HIM! I THINK, "DAMN, HE MUST BE DANCING HIS ASS OFF?" WELL, COME TO FIND OUT, THAT DUMB BASTERD IS IN THE MIDDLE OF THE DANCE FLOOR PISSING! I'M LIKE NO F-ING WAY! ARE YOU KIDDING ME? I GRAB HIS DUMB ASS AND WE ARE OUT OF THERE! WE LEAVE THE DANCE KNOWING COME MONDAY, WE WILL BE HEARING ABOUT IT! SUPRISINGLY, NOTHING EVER CAME ABOUT IT? LUCKY US!

AFRICA

EVERYBODY REMEMBERS CERTAIN PLACES THEY WOULD GO TO UNDERAGE DRINK ON THE WEEKENDS, RIGHT? WE HAD A FEW LIKE "HAWAII" AND "BEER CAN BEACH" BUT OUR FAVORITE AND MOST USED ONE WAS "AFRICA!" NOT QUITE SURE WHY WE STARTED CALLING IT THIS EXCEPT IT HAD A BUNCH OF TREES WITH LONG VINES I GUESS. IT'S FUNNY BECAUSE IT WAS BASICALLY RIGHT ACROSS FROM THE HIGH SCHOOL. YOU COULD LOOK ACROSS THE FREEWAY AND THEIR WAS OUR SCHOOL! IT WAS PRETTY MUCH A BUST TOO BECAUSE IT WAS JUST LIKE A LITTLE HILL YOU COULD DRIVE UP TO GET OFF THE ROAD. IT WAS AT THE END OF A ROAD THAT LED TO A SAW MILL. IT WAS SURROUNDED BY NOTHING BUT PASTURES WITH COWS ROAMING AROUND. THE COPS COULD JUST DRIVE UP ANYTIME AND BUST YOU. THE FUNNY THING IS…THEY NEVER DID!! TALK ABOUT "LIFE LESSONS" LEARNED AT AFRICA! AND SO MANY "FIRSTS" OUT THERE! WE LEARNED A LOT @ AFRICA! WE MUST HAVE SAT OUT THERE AT LEAST 150 TIMES AND DRANK! IT WAS ALWAYS LIKE, "LET'S GET SOME BEER AND HIT AFRICA!" A LOT OF GUYS "BECAME A MAN" FOR THE 1ST TIME AT AFRICA! WITH

THE EXCEPTION OF THE "DRIVE-INN," AFRICA WAS THE PLACE TO TAKE A GIRL! NOBODY CAME OUT THERE AND IF THEY DID, THEY PARKED FAR ENOUGH AWAY FROM YOU THAT YOU COULD STILL "HAVE FUN" WITHOUT BEING ABLE TO SEE WHAT EACH OTHER WAS DOING! AFRICA WAS ALSO A GOOD PLACE TO "BREAK UP" WITH SOMEONE TOO. BECAUSE WHEN YOU GOT DONE SAYING YOU WANTED TO "JUST BE FRIENDS" AND THE OTHER PERSON STARTED CRYING, GOT PISSED AND JUMPED OUT OF THE CAR, THEY HAD THAT LONG ROAD THEY COULD WALK BEFORE YOU DROVE UP BEHIND THEM AND PICKED THEM UP. IT ACTUALLY WORKED OUT GOOD BECAUSE AFTER YOU BROKE UP AND THEN PICKED THEM BACK UP YOU USUALLY FELT BAD FOR THEM, SAID LETS GIVE IT ANOTHER CHANCE AND THEN MADE UP. YOU WERE ALREADY AT "AFRICA" SO YOU JUST HAD TO TURN AROUND, DRIVE BACK TO THE END OF THE ROAD AND START MAKING OUT! THIS HAPPENED A LOT! WITHOUT NAMING NAMES, THERE WAS SOME SERIOUS CHEATING GOING ON OUT AT AFRICA! WE EVEN DISCUSSED POLITICS AT AFRICA! WELL, IF SAYING THE PRESIDENT WAS AN ASS IS DISCUSSING POLITICS THEN WE DID!

I REMEMBER ONE TIME, CODY AND I WERE SHARING A 12 PACK AND WE PROBABLY HAD LIKE ONE EACH LEFT. SO WE ARE TALKING, LISTENING TO THE RADIO WHEN OUT OF NOWHERE, A BIG ASS COW WALKS RIGHT PAST US ON THE ROAD LIKE IT OWNED THE PLACE! SO CODY AND I LOOK AT EACH OTHER AND JUST START CRACKING UP! CODY HAD THIS OLD BLUE DATSUN TRUCK AND HE USED TO THRASH THIS THING! WE BOTH KNEW WHAT THE OTHER ONE WAS THINKING TOO! CODY TAKES OFF DOWN THE HILL, ONTO THE STREET AND STARTS COMING UP ON THE COW. HE GETS BEHIND THE COW AND STARTS GIVING

IT A FEW "BUMPS IN THE ASS." WE ARE ROLLING! THAT COW IS PISSED! HE'S ALL HONKING AND MAKING NOISE! PROBABLY SAYING, "QUIT IT YOU DUMB MOTHER F-ERS!! DOES CODY QUIT? HELL NO! BUMP, BUMP, BUMP HE HITS THE COW IN THE ASS AGAIN! YOU KINDA HAVE TO BE THERE! I KNOW IT SOUNDS CRUEL, BUT WE WERN'T HURTING IT AND GOD WAS IT FUNNY! FINALLY THE COW HAD ENOUGH! HE PULLS OVER TO THE SIDE, CROSSES A DITCH AND JUST LOOKS AT US LIKE, "YOU GUYS ARE ASSHOLES!" FUNNY STUFF! AFRICA RULED!!

THE BIRDS AND THE BEES

GROWING UP IN A FAMILY OF 6 BOYS AND NO SISTERS YOU WOULD THINK THE SUBJECT OF "SEX" AND HAVING BABIES WOULD MOST LIKELY COME UP, RIGHT? WELL NOT IN MY FAMILY! MY DAD DIDN'T SPEAK ON THE SUBJECT, MOM EITHER. I GUESS THEY JUST EXPECTED US TO LEARN ABOUT IT ON OUR OWN! I KNOW A LOT OF FRIENDS WHO'S PARENTS WERE THE SAME WAY! IT JUST WASN'T DISCUSSED LIKE IT IS TODAY! IT'S EVERYWHERE! IN FACT THEY EVEN HAVE COMMERCIALS ABOUT CONDOMS! THAT NEVER WOULD HAVE BEEN TOLERATED!

SO...MY BROTHER DAN AND I LEARNED WHAT WE COULD LISTENING TO OUR OLDER BROTHERS! MAYBE HIDING AROUND A CORNER WHEN THEY WERE TALKING ABOUT HAVING SEX THE NIGHT BEFORE, OR WHAT THEY WANTED TO DO TO THIS GIRL AND THAT GIRL! FOR THE LONGEST TIME WE

THOUGHT SEX WAS SOMETHING YOU DID ON A BASEBALL FIELD! ALWAYS TALKING ABOUT GETTING TO FIRST BASE WITH A GIRL OR SECOND BASE! STUFF LIKE THAT! I KNOW MY BROTHERS WERENT VERY GOOD AT "SEX BASEBALL" THOUGH! BECAUSE ALL THEY EVER TALKED ABOUT WAS GETTING TO FIRST BASE WITH A GIRL. SOMETIMES THEY WOUKD GET A DOUBLE OR GET TO SECOND BASE BUT HARDLY EVER A TRIPLE AND I NEVER HEARD THEM TALKING ABOUT GETTING A HOMERUN! IT WASN'T UNTIL WAY LATER WE FIGURED OUT "THE BASES" AND WHAT THAT MEANT WITH A GIRL! WE WERE SO STUPID! ANYWAY, ONCE IN AWHILE WE WOULD FIND A "PLAYBOY" MAGAZINE IN ONE OF THE OLDER BROTHERS ROOMS. MAN, THOSE GIRLS ALL LIKED SUNSETS AND WALKS ON THE BEACH! REMEMBER, THIS WAS LIKE THE LATE 70'S AND BOY WERE THOSE LADIES HAIRY!! WITH BIG BOOBIES! WE LIKED "PLAYBOY!" OUR MOM ON THE OTHER HAND, DID NOT! MAN WOULD SHE GET MAD WHEN SHE FOUND US LOOKING AT "THE LADIES!"

IT'S FUNNY WHEN I LOOK BACK NOW AND THINK ABOUT HOW BAD I WAS AS A KID! I REMEMBER KISSING GIRLS IN THE 4TH GRADE! ALREADY IN THE 5TH GRADE I KNEW ABOUT "FRENCH KISSING!" IT WAS HARD TO GET A GIRL TO FRENCH KISS IN THE 5TH GRADE; THEY ALL THOUGHT IT WAS GROSS! I KINDA DID TOO, ESPECIALLY WHEN THE GIRLS BREATH WAS BAD! I'M SURE MINE WASN'T MUCH BETTER! BUT I THOUGHT THIS WAS WHAT YOU WERE SUPPOSED TO DO! I EVEN REMEMBER AT RECESS GOING WAY OUT TO THE KICKBALL FIELD, FACING THE SCHOOL SO WE COULD SEE IF A TEACHER WAS COMING AND TRYING TO GET TO 2ND BASE! I LAUGH NOW BECAUSE I THINK IN THE 5TH GRADE I HAD BIGGER BOOBIES THAN THE GIRLS THAT I TRIED TO SEE! THE 6TH GRADE (WHICH

WAS 6TH THROUGH 8TH) MEANT "OLDER WOMAN" AND I THOUGHT I WAS READY! UNTIL ONE DAY AT LUNCHTIME. THERE WAS A GROUP OF US SITTING IN THE MIDDLE OF THE FOOTBALL FIELD JUST TALKING WHEN THIS 8TH GRADE GIRL CAME UP TO ME. I GUESS SHE THOUGHT I WAS CUTE BECAUSE HER FRIENDS KEPT TELLING ME THAT "BECKY" HAD A CRUSH ON ME! DON'T GET ME WRONG, BECKY WAS PRETTY, SHE WAS A 8TH GRADER AND SHE WAS TALL. SHE ALSO HAD PRETTY BIG BOOBS WHICH DIDN'T HURT. ANYWAY, THE ONE DAY SHE CAME UP TO ME, SHE ASKED IF WE COULD GO TALK. I SAID YEAH, AND AS I WAS GETTING UP MY WHOLE GROUP STARTED GOING "WOOOHOOO" "UH OH" JUST GIVING US SHIT! I WAS LIKE, "GROW UP ASSHOLES!" WE WALKED A SHORT WAYS AWAY AND "BECKY" TOLD ME SHE LIKED ME AND HAD LIKED ME FOR AWHILE. I WAS LIKE, OK. THEN SHE ASKED IF SHE COULD GIVE ME A KISS? I WAS LIKE, OH YEAH, "I'M GONNA KISS A 8TH GRADER!" NOW I THOUGHT IT WAS JUST GONNA BE A KISS LIKE A "PECK" ON THE LIPS! SO I CLOSED MY EYES AND LEANED IN. ALL OF A SUDDEN, THE BIGGEST TONGUE IN THE WORLD HAD BROKE THROUGH MY LIPS AND WAS NOW IN MY MOUTH! THIS "BEAST" WAS GOING A MILE A MINUTE IN MY MOUTH AND I THOUGHT IT WAS GOING TO GO DOWN MY THROAT! I COULD BARELY BREATHE! I MEAN, I HAD KISSED A COUPLE GIRLS "FRENCH" BUT ONLY FOR A SECOND OR TWO AND WHEN I DID I THINK I PULLED OUT AS SOON AS OUR TONGUES TOUCHED! NOTHING LIKE THIS MESS! ALL I REMEMBER IS FALLING BACK ON MY ASS, GETTING UP AND RUNNING AS FAST AS I COULD TOWARDS THE CLASSROOMS! LUCKILY THE BELL JUST RANG! I WAS IN SHOCK! I WONDERED WHAT THE HELL "BECKY" JUST DID TO ME? WAS THAT CALLED "GERMAN KISSING" OR "CHINESE KISSING?" I KNEW IT COULDN'T BE "FRENCH" KISSING BECAUSE YOU ONLY TOUCH

TONGUES AND THEN YOU STOP. WELL I AVOIDED "BECKY" EVERY CHANCE I COULD AFTER THAT. I MUST SAY SHE WAS PRETTY COOL ABOUT THE WHOLE THING. SHE COULD HAVE TOLD EVERYONE WHAT A LITTLE "PUSS" I WAS AND HOW I RAN AWAY LIKE A LITTLE BITCH, BUT SHE DIDN'T. EVENTUALLY BEFORE SCHOOL ENDED AND SHE GRADUATED, WE TALKED ABOUT IT! SHE APOLIGIZED FOR SCARING ME AND I SAID SORRY FOR BEING A BABY ABOUT IT! SHE DID GET NICKNAMED "MONSTER TONGUE!" SHE MOVED AWAY THE FOLLOWING YEAR SO NOBODY EVER FOUND OUT ABOUT "MY NIGHTMARE" WITH MONSTER TONGUE! UNTIL NOW THAT IS!!

SIDETRACKED 101

I HAD A SCIENCE TEACHER MY FRESHMAN YEAR AND WE WILL CALL HIM "MR. ATOM." NOW MR. ATOM WAS A SHORT, OLDER GENTLEMAN WHO WAS GOING BALD BUT HAD JUST ENOUGH HAIR TO "FLIP IT" AND DO A COMBOVER. HE HAD BIG "MR. MAGOO" EYEGLASSES AND A LITTLE "HITLER" MOUSTACHE. HE WORE THE SAME SUIT EVERYDAY, EITHER THAT OR HE OWNED 12 SUITS EXACTLY THE SAME! HE HAD A FUNNY LITTLE VOICE. AND AFTER EVERY SENTENCE HE WOUKD SAY, "SEE!" FOR EXAMPLE: HE WOULD SAY, "YOU PEOPLE GOT TO GET TO CLASS ON TIME...SEE!" "I TAKE THE ROLL CALL WHEN THE LAST BELL RINGS...SEE!" DAMN IT WAS FUNNY! ANYWAY, OVER THE YEARS I HAVE HAD MANY FRIENDS WHO WERE IN THAT CLASS WITH ME AND THEY ALWAYS THANK ME FOR "SIDETRACKING" MR. ATOM EVERYDAY AND MAKING THE CLASS FUN!

IT WAS THE SAME THING EVERYDAY, NEVER FAILED! I WOULD ASK HIM THE SAME QUESTIONS EVERY MORNING AND HE WOULD ANSWER THEM LIKE

IT WAS THE FIRST TIME THEY WERE EVER ASKED! EVERYDAY! IT WOULD GO LIKE THIS! MR. ATOM, WHATS BEHIND THAT DOOR RIGHT BEHIND YOU? HE WOULD TURN AROUND, LOOK AT THE DOOR, TURN BACK AROUND AND SAY: "THAT'S A LITTLE OFFICE BACK THERE, SEE. IT'S GOT A SINK WITH RUNNING WATER AND A LITTLE FRIDGE, SEE. THAT'S WHERE I EAT MY LUNCH, SEE. THEN I WOULD SAY, MR. ATOM, WHERE DO YOU EAT LUNCH? HE WOULD SAY, THERES A LITTLE OFFICE BACK THERE SEE, I EAT MY LUNCH BACK IN THAT OFFICE, SEE. ONE DAY HE TOLD US HE HAD SOME CHICKENS AND ROOSTERS. SO I WOULD SAY, MR. ATOM, DO YOU HAVE ANY PETS? HE WOULD SAY, OH NOT REALLY, SEE. BUT I DO HAVE BANNY ROOSTERS, SEE. I ALSO HAVE THESE LITTLE CHICKS (AND HE WOULD GIVE THE PROPER NAME OF THEM BUT I FORGET WHAT IT WAS) AND THEY HAVE FEATHERS THAT LOOK LIKE THEY ARE WEARING LITTLE SOCKS,SEE. THEN HE WOULD CRACK A QUICK SMILE, WHICH HE NEVER DID!! THIS WOULD GO ON FOR AT LEAST HALF THE CLASS IF NOT LONGER. BY THE TIME WE GOT TO THE LESSON PLAN, THE BELL WOULD RING! I TAKE FULL RESPONSIBILITY FOR MY CLASSMATES NOT LEARNING MUCH SCIENCE OUR FRESHMAN YEAR BUT IT WAS A CLASS THEY REMEMBER!

OH, ONE MORE QUICK ONE BEFORE I FORGET. A COUPLE YEARS LATER I NEEDED TO TAKE ANOTHER SCIENCE CLASS TO GRADUATE AND I WAS ABLE TO TAKE A "EASY" ONE LIKE "ANIMAL SCIENCE" OR SOMETHING. ANYWAY, I HAD CODY IN MY CLASS AND I'M SURE THIS WAS LIKE CHEMISTRY TO HIM (HE STRUGGLED IN SCHOOL) BECAUSE SCHOOL CAME HARD TO CODY! ANYWAY, WE USED TO DO THE "SIDETRACK" THING IN THIS CLASS TO. THE TEACHER, LETS CALL HIM "MR. FARMER" WAS A SWEET MAN! HE WAS THE NICEST GUY! REALLY INVOLVED IN LITTLE

LEAGUE, HAD OLDER KIDS WHO PLAYED SPORTS, JUST A GOOD DAD! WELL OF COURSE CODY AND I DID NO WORK IN THAT CLASS EXCEPT WRITE A FEW REPORTS. ALWAYS "IN CLASS" BECAUSE WE DIDN'T DO HOMEWORK! WE DIDN'T REALLY THINK OR CARE ABOUT GRADES UNTIL RIGHT BEFORE REPORT CARD TIME. THE TEACHERS WOULD TELL YOU WHAT YOU WERE GONNA BE GETTING AHEAD OF TIME SO IF ANYTHING WAS MISSING YOU WOULD HAVE TIME TO MAKE IT UP! WELL I REMEMBER ONE REPORT CARD TIME, CODY AND I WERE TOLD WE WERE GETTING F'S! WE WERE SHOCKED! I DON'T KNOW WHY, WE DIDN'T DO THE WORK! MY DAD WAS GOING TO KILL ME BECAUSE HERE HE WAS A TEACHER AND HIS KID IS GETTING AN "F"! PLUS I NEVER HAD HOMEWORK! CODY PLAYED ON THE SCHOOLS BASEBALL TEAM AND IF HE GOT AN "F" THEN HE WOULD BE KICKED OFF! SO WE STAYED AFTER CLASS AND SPOKE TO MR. FARMER ABOUT OUR GRADES. HE FELT BAD AND WAS APOLIGIZING FOR HAVING TO GIVE US AN "F"! WE GOT ALL SAD AND TOLD HIM THAT WE WERE DOING OK IN OUR OTHER CLASSES BUT JUST HAD TROUBLE IN HIS! WE SAID IT CAME HARD TO US. WE THEN TOLD HIM THAT WE BOTH JUST HAD TO HAVE AT LEAST C'S OR WE WERE BOTH GONNA GET KICKED OFF THE BASEBALL TEAM. REMEMBER, CODY PLAYS BASEBALL, NOT ME! HE THOUGHT IT OVER AND OVER AND THEN HE WAS LIKE, "WELL BOYS, WE CAN'T HAVE YOU NOT PLAYING BASEBALL!": I TELL YOU WHAT, YOU EACH WRITE ME A ONE PAGE REPORT ON THE ANIMAL OF YOUR CHOICE AND YOU WILL GET YOUR C'S! WE WERE HIGH FIVING MR. FARMER, PATTING HIM ON THE BACK JUST MAKING TONS OF NOISE! YOU WOULD HAVE THOUGHT WE WON THE WORLD SERIES! HE WAS SO HAPPY AND PROUD OF HIMSELF! MADE US FEEL GOOD THAT WE COULD BRING SO MUCH JOY TO HIS LIFE! WE GOT C'S!!

BEER AND DANCING

THE DANCES WERE ALWAYS AN EXCITING TIME IN OUR JOURNEY THROUGH ADOLESCENCE. ESPECIALLY THE "JUNIOR HIGH" DANCES AT YUBA GARDENS SCHOOL! THE ULTIMATE GOAL WAS TO "HOOK UP" WITH A CUTE GIRL BY THE END OF THE DANCE. WHAT I MEAN BY "HOOKING UP" WAS NO MORE THAN A MAKE-OUT SESSION IN THE MIDDLE OF THE DANCE FLOOR BY THE LAST SLOW SONG OF THE NIGHT!

THE ENTIRE NIGHT WAS SPENT ON TESTING THE WATERS TO SEE WHO MIGHT BE "GAME" AND TO RULE OUT THE "TIGHT ONES" WHO WEREN'T QUITE READY! WE ONLY HAD A FEW HOURS SO TIME WAS OF THE ESSENCE!

THROUGHOUT THE NIGHT, WE WOULD HAVE THE "FAST" DANCE SONGS TO SHOWCASE OUR GOOD MOVES AND CATCH THE EYE OF THE LADIES! BUT WE DIDN'T WANT TO GET TO SWEATY AND "AXE" WASN'T INVENTED YET! WE STILL HAD THE SLOW SONGS TO THINK ABOUT! THERE WAS A KEY PART OF THE "INTERVIEW PROCESS" IN NARROWING DOWN THE LIST OF CANDIDATES WHO MAY RECEIVE THAT LASTING SMOOCH! THROUGHOUT A SLOW DANCE, WHILE AVOIDING THE CHAPERONES WHO WERE CONSTANTLY WALKING AROUND, WE HAD TO SEE HOW LOW WE COULD GET OUR HANDS ON THEIR ASSES BEFORE THEY GRABBED THEM AND PULLED THEM BACK UP TO THEIR WAIST! THIS LASTED ALL NIGHT. ONCE IN A GREAT WHILE YOU WOULD GET A GIRL WHO WOULD LET YOU LEAVE YOUR HANDS THERE! SCORE! BUT NOT OFTEN!!

ONE PARTICULAR DANCE, CALLED THE 8TH GRADE GRADUATION DANCE, DAN REALLY FELT THE NEED TO "ENHANCE" THE SITUATION. HE HAD A GIRL THAT HE LIKED, WHO LIVED RIGHT ACROSS THE STREET FROM THE SCHOOL. HER MOM LOVED TO HAVE THE OCCASSIONAL "SIP" OF THE VODKA! THEY DECIDED TO SNEAK OFF IN THE MIDDLE OF THE DANCE TO JOIN HER IN A COUPLE "CHUGS!" IT WAS AWESOME! AFTER PARTYING FOR A FEW MINUTES, THEY WENT BACK TO THE DANCE AND ALL WAS GOOD IN THE WORLD!

FAST FORWARD TO FRESHMAN YEAR (DAN'S) AT LINDHURST HIGH SCHOOL. THE DANCES BY THIS TIME HAD LOST THEIR LUSTER! NOTHING COMPARED TO THE JUNIOR HIGH DANCES. I DON'T KNOW IF WE JUST HAD BETTER THINGS TO DO OR THEY JUST WEREN'T FUN ANYMORE. IT MAY HAVE TO DO WITH

ONE PARTICULAR DANCE THAT WAS OVER BEFORE IT STARTED!

DAN, JOE AND RONALD DECIDED TO GO TO ONE PARTICULAR DANCE, BUT NOT BEFORE GETTING SOMEONE TO "BUY" ALCOHOL FOR US. IT WASN'T UNTIL WE WERE LIKE 19 YRS OLD WHEN WE WERE ABLE TO PASS FOR 21 AND BUY BEER FOR OURSELVES. WE PAYED SOME RANDOM ADULT THEIR "FEE" FOR BUYING US THE BEER AND WE PUT DOWN THE 12 PACK IN A MATTER OF MINUTES! WE ONLY LIVED A HOP, SKIP AND A JUMP FROM THE HIGH SCHOOL.

AS THE THREE OF US ATTEMPTED TO GO IN, MARGE OR "SARGE" THE LADY SECURITY GUARD FOR THE SCHOOL STOPPED US. SHE HAD A "NOSE" ON HER! SHE SMELLED THE BEER ON US FROM A MILE AWAY! YOU COULDN'T GET ANYTHING OVER ON MARGE! WE WERE SO DUMB AND DIDN'T EVEN THINK ABOUT CHEWING SOME GUM OR SOMETHING FOR THE BREATHE! STUPID FRESHMAN!

WE WERE TAKEN AWAY TO THE PRINCIPAL'S OFFICE, OUR PARENTS WERE CALLED DOWN TO THE SCHOOL AND THAT WAS THAT! SUSPENDED FROM SCHOOL FOR A WEEK, KICKED OFF THE BASEBALL TEAM AND GETTING THE STARE DOWN AND "I'M ASHAMED OF YOU" LOOKS FROM OUR PARENTS, PRICELESS!! JOE HAD IT EASY, HIS PARENTS NEVER GOT TOO UPSET! GO FIGURE. "SARGE" WON THAT BATTLE!!

THAT RED TRUCK

JACK WAS ALWAYS TINKERING AROUND WITH VEHICLES. WHEN WE ALL WANTED TO GO OUT AND GET ROWDY, JACK WOULD HAVE THE HOOD UP ON SOME CAR THAT HE WAS PERSISTANT ABOUT GETTING FIXED AND HE WASN'T STOPPING UNTIL HE FOUND THE PROBLEM!
ONE PARTICULAR VEHICLE HE WAS FOND OF WAS HIS 67 CHEVY TRUCK! HE LOVED THAT THING SO MUCH. HE PAINTED IT CANDY RED. HE WAS OBSESSED WITH TWEAKING THE ENGINE TO PERFECTION!

IT NEVER FAILED, THAT AFTER SHOOTING DOWN A FEW BEERS OUT AT "AFRICA" WE WOULD HIT THE FREEWAY TO SEE IF THIS WAS GOING TO BE THE TIME THAT WE HIT THE "MAGIC 100 MPH!" AFTER MANY ATTEMPTS AND LONG HOURS THAT TURNED INTO DAYS, MONTHS AND EVEN YEARS OF TURNING THAT WRENCH, YES IT DID! THE GUAGE FINALLY HIT THE MAGIC NUMBER AND WE WERE SO FIRED UP, IT WAS TIME TO PARTY! NOW WHO REALLY KNOWS IF THE SPEEDOMETER EVEN WORKED CORRECTLY? THERE WAS ALWAYS SOMETHING WRONG WITH THAT

TRUCK! I DON'T KNOW HOW MANY TIMES WE RAN OUT OF GAS AND HAD TO PUSH THAT DAMN THING BECAUSE THE GAS GUAGE WAS BROKE!

THEN, THERE WAS THE TIME THAT JACK AND DAN WERE AT A "RAGING HOUSE PARTY" THAT GOT BROKEN UP BY THE SOUNDS OF SIRENS. IT WAS RAINING LIKE "CATS AND DOGS" AND JACK HAULED ASS OUT OF THERE BEFORE THE COPS CAME. PROBLEM WAS, HIS WIPERS DIDN'T WORK! SEE, SOMETHING WAS ALWAYS WRONG WITH IT! ANYWAY, DAN WOULD HAVE TO REACH AROUND, OUT THE PASSENGER WINDOW AND MANUALLY MOVE THE WIPER UP AND DOWN, WHICH WOULD SOME HOW MOVE THE DRIVER'S WIPER EVERY 3RD TIME. DAN WAS SOAKING WET AND DIRTY BUT HEY, THEY COULD SEE!

THAT';S WHAT I'M TALKING ABOUT…SOME WIRE WAS HOOKED TO ANOTHER WIRE, TAPED TO ANOTHER, WHICH WAS. WELL, YOU GET THE POINT!! "WHITE TRASH VEHICLE!"

8TH GRADE TRIP

OUR SCHOOL WAS HEADING TO SAN FRANCISCO FOR THE END OF THE YEAR TRIP. WE WOULD BE GRADUATING IN A MONTH, AND THIS WAS OUR REWARD FOR A YEAR WELL DONE!

THIS WAS ALSO ABOUT THE TIME THE "DRINKING ADVENTURES" WERE ABOUT TO BEGIN FOR DAN, JOE, JACK AND RONALD!

THE TRIP WAS HEAVILY CHAPPERONED WITH TEACHERS. THEY WERE ASSIGNED TO KIDS WHO WERE TOLD REPEATEDLY TO "STAY IN YOUR ASSIGNED GROUPS!" HELL, WE WERE IN SAN FRANCISCO! WELL, THAT WASN'T GOOD ENOUGH FOR US! WE MADE A GROUP DECISION TO WANDER OFF AND MAKE OUR OWN ADVENTURES. NOT THE ASSIGNED, WELL MAPPED OUT AGENDA OF VISITING THE PLANATARIAM OR THE EXPLORATORIUM! WE HAD OUR OWN EXPLORING TO DO!

THEY WENT UP AND DOWN THE "STREETS OF SAN FRANCISCO", HUNG WITH THE "STREET PEOPLE" AND JUST TOOK IN THE "CULTURE OF THE CITY!" "YOU

KNOW WHAT WOULD MAKE THIS TRIP EVEN BETTER, JACK SUGGESTED?" BEER!! WITH A SLIGHT HESITATION, WE ALL AGREED! LET'S DO THIS. BUT HOW?

IT DIDN'T TAKE LONG. THEY SAW A BUM SITTING OUTSIDE A LIQUOR STORE. THEY GROUPED THEIR MONEY TOGETHER AND ASKED THE BUM TO BUY THEM A 6-PACK OF COORS TALL CANS. I REMEMBER TO THIS DAY. HOW DID THEY KNOW TO ASK FOR "TALL CANS?" THE BUM GOT TO KEEP THE CHANGE. HE WAS HAPPY! THEY WERE HAPPY, EVERYONE WAS HAPPY! THEY FOUND A ALLEY WAY WHERE THEY GUZZLED DOWN THE 16 OUNCERS AS FAST AS THEY COULD! "TAKE IT TO THE HEAD!" MAN DID THEY CATCH A BUZZ!

EVENTUALLY THEY MADE IT BACK TO THE MEETING AREA WHERE IT WAS TIME TO HOP IN THE BUS AND HEAD HOME.

THEY TOLD SO MANY PEOPLE ON THE RIDE HOME. THEY FELT LIKE THEY GOT AWAY WITH MURDER! I STILL TO THIS DAY DON'T KNOW HOW IT DIDN'T GET BACK TO THE FACUILTY?!

A NIGHT IN HAWAII

MANY PARTIES TOOK PLACE OUT IN THIS PLACE CALLED "HAWAII." THIS WAS AN OLD "BACKROAD" ABOUT 5 MILES OUTSIDE OF MARYSVILLE. THIS IS A PLACE WHERE "KEGGERS" HAPPENED! THIS AREA WAS USED PRIMARLY BY THE RIVAL MARYSVILLE HIGH SCHOOL STUDENTS (WE HAD "AFRICA") BUT WE WOULD SHOW UP AT THE FIRST HINT OF A PARTY, INVITED OR NOT!

ON ONE PARTICULAR NIGHT JACK AND DAN HITCHED A RIDE WITH THE "JACKSON TWINS" OUT TO HAWAII. BASICALLY,JUST INVITED OURSELVES TO THE PARTY. WE DIDN'T REALLY KNOW ANYONE BUT JUST TRIED TO BLEND IN THE BEST AS WE COULD. THINGS WERE GOING GOOD SO FAR. THEN, FROM A MILE AWAY YOU COULD SEE THE "FLASHING LIGHTS!" NO LESS THAN 6 COP CARS SHOWED UP! THEY ARE LINING PEOPLE UP, CUFFING SOME AND LETTING SOME GO. JACK AND DAN HAD THIS GREAT IDEA TO JUMP INTO THE HEAVILY VEGITATED DITCHES THAT CONSUMED BOTH SIDES OF THE ROAD.

AFTER AVOIDING ARREST AND DODGING THE FLASHLIGHT THAT SEARCHED THE DITCHES, IT BECAME QUIET. AS DAN "POPPED" HIS HEAD UP TO TAKE A LOOK, HE LUCKED OUT TO FIND THAT EVERYONE WAS GONE! NO COPS, NO CARS, NOBODY! HE WAS BUMMED THOUGH BECAUSE HE AND JACK GOT SEPERATED DURING THE BUST AND HE WAS ALL ALONE. SUDDENLY, FROM THE OPPOSITE SIDE OF THE ROAD, JACK'S HEAD POPPED UP. BOY WAS DAN HAPPY TO SEE HIM! HE WAS REUNITED WITH HIS FRIEND!

THEY STARTED THE LONG WALK BACK TO TOWN, AS DIRTY AS EVER (HMMM...WHITE TRASH?) WHEN ALL OF A SUDDEN HEADLIGHTS APPEAR. AS THEY WERE PREPARED TO JUMP BACK IN THE DITCH, THEY NOTICED THAT THESE WERE NO "POLICE CAR HEADLIGHTS!" IT HAPPENED TO BE A TRUCK COMING BACK OUT THERE. WHO ARE THESE GUYS THEY WONDERED? THIS WASN'T THE RIDE THEY CAME OUT HERE WITH! THEY DIDN'T KNOW THESE GUYS! JACK AND DAN WERE THINKING A FIGHT WAS ABOUT TO HAPPEN. BEING DRUNK AND DIRTY, THEY WERE AS READY AS THEY WOULD EVER BE.

THE TRUCK PULLED UP, TWO GUYS JUMP OUT OF THE CAB AND TWO OUT OF THE BACK OF THE TRUCK. COME TO FIND OUT THEY WERE JUST THERE TO PICK UP A KEG THEY STASHED IN THE DITCH DURING THE BUST! DAMN, IF JACK AND DAN KNEW THERE WAS A KEG THERE THEY WOULD HAVE BEEN JUST FINE!

AT LEAST THESE "MARYSVILLE GUYS" WERE COOL ENOUGH TO GIVE THE GUYS A RIDE BACK TO TOWN! THEY GOT DROPPED OFF AT "JACK IN THE BOX." HUNGRY AND DIRTY, THEY TRIED TO ORDER

SOME FOOD THROUGH THE "DRIVE THRU" WHERE THEY WERE DENIED FOR NOT HAVING A VEHICLE. PLUS, THEY WERE LOOKING "PRETTY!" THEY STILL TO THIS DAY DON'T REMEMBER HOW THEY EVENTUALLY GOT BACK HOME THAT NIGHT/MORNING, WHICH WAS A GOOD 7 MILES AWAY! THEY THINK THEY MUST HAVE CALLED SOMEONE ON THE PAYPHONE BECAUSE "CELL PHONES" HAD NOT YET BEEN BORN!

IT'S HOT AS HELL

BEING FORTUNATE TO LIVE IN NORTHERN CALIFORNIA, WE HAVE "GREAT" SUMMERS! HOWEVER, SOMEDAYS ARE JUST "TOO DAMN HOT!" WE WERE NOT FORTUNATE ENOUGH TO KNOW MANY FRIENDS WHO HAD POOLS AND THE ONES WHO DID FIGURED OUT PRETTY FAST THAT WE JUST WANTED TO USE THEIR POOL. THEY ALWAYS WONDERED WHY THEY HAD SO MANY MORE "FRIENDS" AROUND SUMMERTIME!

WE WOULD SOMETIMES GET LUCKY AND OUR MOM WOULD GIVE US ENOUGH MONEY TO GO DOWN TO THE "OLIVEHURST POOL." I THINK SHE JUST GOT TIRED OF US LAYING AROUND THE HOUSE, ALL LAYED OUT LIKE WE WERE DYING FROM THE HEAT. SO WHAT BETTER WAY TO GET THE HOUSE TO HERSELF! SO WE WOULD GO TO THE POOL BUT IT WAS KINDA GROSS! THEY MADE YOU STEP IN THIS SOLUTION BEFORE YOU GOT IN THE POOL AND IT ALWAYS

LOOKED AND FELT BAD!! THEN WE ALWAYS HEARD PEOPLE PEE'D IN THE POOL! I KNOW I DID A COUPLE TIMES! WHY STOP A GREAT GAME OF "MARCO POLO" JUST TO PISS! ONE OF THE GOOD THINGS ABOUT GOING THERE WAS THIS GREAT LOOKING LIFEGUARD! SHE WORE THIS RED BATHING SUIT AND SWEAR TO GOD SHE LOOKED LIKE "FARRAH FAWCETT!" SHE WOULD SIT UP ON THE LIFEGUARD STAND AND WATCH ALL US LITTLE SHIT'S TRY NOT TO DROWN! IF YOU GOT CAUGHT RUNNING OR TRYING TO "DUNK" YOUR BUDDY YOU WOULD GET PUT UNDER THE LIFEGUARD STAND (LIKE A TIMEOUT) FOR LIKE 10-15 MINUTES! WE WOULD GET CAUGHT ON PURPOSE BECAUSE THEN WE COULD LOOK UP AND TRY TO SEE BETWEEN HER LEGS! WE NEVER SAW ANYTHING BUT KIDS WOULD SWEAR THEY SAW EVERYTHING!! LYING LITTLE SHIT'S!! WE TALKED A BIG GAME!

WHEN WE COULDN'T GO TO THE POOL, WE WOULD MAKE OUR OWN "SLIP AND SLIDES!" I KNOW A LOT OF YOU HAVE DONE THIS SO DON'T ACT LIKE YOU ALWAYS HAD "STORE BOUGHT" SLIP AND SLIDES BY "WHAMMO!" YOU WOULD TAKE TRASH BAGS (50 GALLON USUALLY) AND CUT THEM UP THE SIDES TO MAKE 1 LONG PIECE OF PLASTIC. THEN YOU WOULD PUT LIKE 3-4 OF THESE THINGS LONGWAYS TO MAKE ONE BIG SLIDE. WE WOULD HAVE LIKE ROCKS HOLDING THE SLIDE DOWN WHILE SOMEONE WOULD GET THE HOSE AND SOAK THE SHIT OUT OF THE PLASTIC. THEN YOU WOULD LINE UP, RUN LIKE HELL AND DO A "PETE ROSE" SLIDE AND SEE IF YOU COULD MAKE IT TO THE END! THIS USUALLY LASTED ABOUT A HALF HOUR IF WE WERE LUCKY! THE PLASTIC WOULD RIP OR IT WOULD BE LAYING ON TOP OF SHARP ROCKS YOU NEVER SAW AND AS YOU SLID IT WOULD CUT THE SHIT OUT OF THE PLASTIC...AND YOU! PLUS, EVERYTIME SOMEONE SLID YOU WOULD HAVE TO

WAIT WHILE IT GOT ENOUGH WATER BACK ON IT FOR THE NEXT GUY! NOT TO MENTION WHAT IT DID TO THE GRASS UNDERNEATH! OUR DAD WOULD COME HOME AND SEE OUR LAWN AND BE READY TO KICK THE SHIT OUT OF US! "LOOK WHAT YOU DID TO THE LAWN" HE'D YELL! "YOU BETTER FIND ANOTHER WAY TO KEEP COOL!" THEN WE WOULD SAY, "YOU GOT MONEY FOR THE POOL THEN?" HELL NO, GO ASK YOUR MOM! GREAT!

I REMEMBER ONE SUMMER, EVERY HOUSE GOT DELIVERED THE NEW PLASTIC "TOTES" (GARBAGE CANS) FROM YSDI (YUBA SUTTER DISPOSAL) AND ONE OF US HAD THE GREAT IDEA OF MAKING THESE OUR OWN PERSONAL "JACUZZI'S!" WE WOULD FILL THESE THINGS WITH WATER AND THEN GET A LADDER AND TRY TO JUMP IN WITHOUT KNOCKING IT OVER. IF YOU DID, YOU WOULD HAVE TO REFILL THE DAMN THING! THIS WAS FUN FOR LIKE 10 MINUTES. YOU COULD BARELY MOVE BECAUSE THERE WAS NO ROOM! PLUS YOUR "JACUZZI" ONLY HAD BUBBLES WHEN WE FARTED AND THAT GOT OLD PRETTY QUICK! THE FUNNIEST ONES WERE THAT OF THE KIDS WHO DIDN'T CLEAN OUT THEIR TOTES BEFORE THEY FILLED THEM UP TO "SWIM!" THEY'D HAVE ALL THIS SHIT FLOATING IN THEIR "JACUZZI" LIKE WRAPPERS, CANS, OLD FOOD! NICE! HEY, WE WERE "WHITE TRASH" AND WE TRIED TO STAY "COOL" BY ANY MEANS NECCESARY!!

LET IT SNOW

LIVING WHERE WE DID MEANT THAT WE COULD GET TO THE SNOW PRETTY EASY. ALOT OF PEOPLE LIKE TO SNOW SKI AND WOULD TRAVEL TOWARDS RENO. THEY WOULD GO TO "SUGAR BOWL" OR "BOREAL." HOWEVER, WHEN YOU'RE A KID WITH NO MONEY YOU DON'T REALLY GET INTO SKIING! MORE LIKE "FREE SPORTS!" WE USED TO DRIVE TO A TOWN NAMED LAPORTE. YOU GET THERE AND THE ROAD JUST STOPS. BLOCKED WITH SNOW, YOU CAN DRIVE NO FURTHER! YEP, THIS IS THE PLACE. IT HAD GREAT BIG HILLS TO RIDE DOWN WITH HUGE "DROP OFFS!" THE SHOW "JACKASS" HAD NOTHING ON US! IN FACT, WE WERE DOING JACKASS TYPE STUNTS WHEN BAM MAGERA WAS STILL IN DIAPERS! WE WOULD TRY AND FIND ANYTHING THAT WOULD SLIDE DOWN THE SLOPES GOOD. IF WE COULD FIND OUR OLD

"SAUCERS" FROM THE YEAR BEFORE WE WERE LUCKY! MOSTLY THOUGH WE JUST USED CARDBOARD! IT ACTUALLY HELD UP PRETTY GOOD IF YOU GOT SOME STURDY PIECES FROM LIKE FURNITURE OR SOMETHING. ONE OF THE MOST MEMORABLE TRIPS TO THE SNOW WAS THE TIME THAT JACK USED (AND GOT SCREAMED AT AND PROBABLY BEATEN) HIS MOM'S "IRONING BOARD!" JACK HAD THE GREAT IDEA OF SNAPPING THE LEGS OFF OF IT AND USING IT AS A SLED! HE WAS THE "GENIUS" OF THE BUNCH! WE COULDN'T WAIT TO TRY OUT OUR "NEW SNOWBOARD!" BY THE TIME WE ARRIVED WE WERE FEELING NO PAIN! MANY BEERS AND A BOTTLE OF "SHNAPP'S" HAD BEEN CONSUMED! WE ALL HAD TO MAKE "YELLOW SNOW" THEN WE WERE READY TO RIDE! WANTING TO TRY OUT HIS "NEW INVENTION" JACK STARTED RUNNING DOWN THE ROAD (WHICH WAS ALL ICED OVER FROZEN) THEN HE DOVE OUT ON HIS "IRONING BOARD SLED" AND MISJUDGED IT BY A FOOT, SLAMMING HIS FACE INTO THE ICY ROAD AND SLIDING A COUPLE FEET, FACE FIRST. JACK WORE BRACES ON HIS TEETH AND WHEN HE GOT UP HE HAD WIRES POKING OUT ALL OVER HIS MOUTH WHICH WAS A "BLOODY MESS!" BEING THE TOUGH BASTARD THAT HE WAS, HE FOUND A SIDE VIEW MIRROR ON A CAR, PUSHED THE WIRES BACK INTO PLACE THE BEST HE COULD AND WE ALL SPREAD OUT LOOKING FOR THE BEST HILL TO CONQUER! WE FOUND SOME PRETTY GOOD ONES! I REMEMBER GOING DOWN THIS HILL WITH LIKE A 10 FOOT DROP AT THE BOTTOM. I WAS FLYING DOWN IT ON CARDBOARD THEN I HIT "THE DROP" AND IT KNOCKED THE AIR OUT OF ME! CODY WAS STANDING RIGHT BY ME JUST LAUGHING AT ME AND MAKING "WHINCING" SOUNDS, SAYING "GET UP YOU LITTLE BITCH!" WHAT A DICK! ☺

NEXT THING WE KNOW, JACK IS SCREAMING AT US TO HURRY UP AND COME OVER TO WHERE HE WAS. HE WAS THERE WITH JOE AND DAN. SOMETHING WAS WRONG. WE RAN OVER TO WHERE THEY WERE STANDING. THEY FOUND A FROZEN OVER POND WHERE THEY WERE TRYING OUT THE IRONING BOARD. I GUESS DAN HAD MISJUDGED HIS DIVE ONTO THE ICE AND INSTEAD OF THE BOARD HITTING THE ICE FIRST, DAN'S CHIN DID (SIMILAR TO WHAT JACK HAD DID EARLIER) AND IT WAS BLEEDING ALL OVER! IT LOOKED LIKE A PIECE OF CHEWED UP MEAT WAS JUST HANGING THERE! GROSS! THE 2 GOOD THINGS HE HAD GOING FOR HIM WAS THAT IT WAS "COLD AS HELL" AND HE WAS STILL BUZZING PRETTY GOOD SO HE DIDN'T FEEL ANYTHING. PART OF THE REASON IT OPENED UP SO BAD WAS THAT DAN HAD CUT HIS CHIN OPEN DURING A FOOTBALL GAME (THE VERY SAME SPOT) AND IT NEVER DID HEAL REAL GOOD. SO WE DROVE BACK TO MARYSVILLE, TOOK HIM TO THE RIDEOUT "ER" AND GOT HIM ALL STITCHED UP! ITS AMAZING THAT HE DIDN'T GET A BAD INFECTION BECAUSE WHEN WE COULDN'T FIND ANYTHING TO HOLD ON DAN'S CHIN TO STOP THE BLEEDING, TROY (ANOTHER FRIEND THAT CAME WITH US) TOOK OFF ONE OF HIS SOCKS (HE WAS WEARING 2 PAIR) WHICH WAS SO SWEATY, DIRTY AND STINKY AND GAVE IT TO DAN TO STOP THE BLEEDING. HE STILL HAS A LITTLE "REMINDER" SCAR THERE TODAY!

MAKE YOURSELF AT HOME

CODY AND DAN BOUGHT A 12 PACK ONE DAY (WELL THEY GOT SOMEBODY TO BUY FOR THEM) AND THEY NEEDED SOMEWHERE TO DRINK IT AT! THEY DECIDED TO GO TO JOE AND JACK'S HOUSE TO KICK BACK AND DRINK. THIS WAS BEFORE THEY GOT THE "LOVE SHACK" (THE TRAILER FROM HELL). SO THEY GO TO THE DOOR AND THEY ARE KNOCKING AND KNOCKING WITH NO ANSWER SO THEY SAID SCREW IT! THEY DECIDED TO TRY THE DOOR AND IT WAS UNLOCKED SO THEY JUST WENT RIGHT IN. NOBODY WAS HOME I GUESS SO THEY FIGURED THEY WOULD JUST WATCH TV AND DRINK LONG ENOUGH TO FINISH THE 12 PACK AND THEN TAKE OFF BEFORE ANYONE GOT HOME! PRETTY BALLSY, I KNOW! WELL THEY ARE HAVING A GOOD TIME WATCHING THE GIANTS PLAY THE BRAVES ON TV, THEY ARE SLAMMING BEERS, SHARING FUNYUNS, GOOD TIMES! WHEN ALL OF A SUDDEN, OUT OF THE CORNER OF THEIR EYES THEY SEE SOMEONE OR SOMETHING COMING AROUND THE CORNER! IT'S MR. JOHNSON! I GUESS HE WAS TAKING

A NAP? THEY NEVER THOUGHT TO CHECK THE BACK ROOMS WHEN THEY CAME IN! OH SHIT! THE THING IS, MR. JOHNSON HAD LOST 90% OFF HIS EYESIGHT AND WAS PRETTY MUCH BLIND! HE COULD SEE FUZZY IMAGES OF YOU BUT COULDNT MAKE OUT FACES! SO HE SITS DOWN AND STARTS "LISTENING" TO THE BALLGAME AND ASKING "JOE:" QUESTIONS, ONLY JOE IS NOT THERE! SO CODY STARTS TALKING LIKE JOE AND ANSWERING "HIS DAD." DAN IS JUST BUSTING UP! NOT ONLY IS HE "BUZZING" BUT THEY WERE GETTING ONE OVER ON MR. JOHNSON! THIS GOES ON FOR LIKE A HALF HOUR MORE THEN THEY FINISH THE BEER. THEY GET READY TO LEAVE AND CODY (WHO'S ACTING LIKE JOE) SAY'S," OK DAD, DAN AND I GOTTA GO BUT I"LL BE BACK IN A FEW HOURS!" THEN MR. JOHNSON SAYS,"YOU AIN'T GOING ANYWHERE UNTIL YOU CLEAN UP THAT GODDAMN ROOM OF YOURS!" I'VE BEEN TELLING YOU, YOUR MOM'S BEEN TELLING YOU BUT DO YOU LISTEN? HELL NO, YOU JUST DO WHATEVER YOU DAMN WELL FEEL LIKE! I DON'T CARE IF YOU'RE FRIENDS HERE OR NOT! OH SHIT! JOE'S NOT EVEN HERE!! WE HAD TO THINK OF SOMETHING FAST! CODY (JOE) SAY'S OK DAD, I'LL GO CLEAN IT UP! "IT'S A MESS!" HEY MR. JOHNSON, "YOU WANT A BEER WHILE I WAIT FOR JOE?" HE THINKS FOR A MINUTE AND SAYS OK. THEN HE SAYS,"I WASN'T GETTING MAD AT YOU DAN, IT'S THAT LAZY ASS JOE!" I KNOW MR. JOHNSON, "NO BIG DEAL!" SO CODY GOES TO THE FRIDGE, OPENS IT AND "DAMN!" IT'S LIKE A JUNGLE IN THERE! SHIT FLYING AROUND, PACKS OF MEAT MOVING, ETC. HE GRABS THE LAST BEER. THE CAN IS ALL DENTED, IT'S EXPIRED BUT HEY ONLY THE BEST FOR MR. JOHNSON! ☺ AS I'M SITTING THERE "BULLSHITTING" WITH JOE'S DAD, CODY COMES SNEAKING AROUND THE CORNER AND INTO THE KITCHEN. NOW IF HE CAN MAKE IT IN TO THE GARAGE, WE GOT IT MADE! AS CODY OPENS THE BACK DOOR

INTO THE GARAGE, THEIR LITTLE WEINER DOG (SALLY) STARTS BARKING HER DAMN HEAD OFF! PANIC!! CODY GRABS A BAG OF CHIPS OFF THE KITCHEN TABLE AND PUTS THEM ON THE FLOOR. THIS SEEMS TO SHUT SALLY UP! NOW CODY MAKES HIS WAY INTO THE GARAGE AND OUT THE BACK DOOR! THAT WAS CLOSE! NOW I GOTTA GO! I SAY, "MR. JOHNSON, I GOTTA GO BUT CAN YOU TELL JOE THAT I WILL CALL HIM TONIGHT?" HE SAY'S, "NO PROBLEM DAN!" THEN I GET UP AND LEAVE! WE MEET AROUND THE CORNER AND JUST START BUSTING UP! "I CAN'T BELIEVE WE TRICKED MR. JOHNSON!" WE SAW JOE THE NEXT DAY AND HE SAYS, "MY DAD IS LOSING IT!" WE GO "WHY, WHAT HAPPENED?"   JOE SAYS, "HE SAYS THAT YOU (POINTING TO DAN) ME AND MY DAD WERE ALL WATCHING THE GIANT'S GAME" THEN HE SAYS HE TOLD ME TO CLEAN MY ROOM AND THAT I COULDN'T LEAVE UNTIL IT WAS DONE. "I WASN'T EVEN HOME!" THEN HE SAID YOU HAD TO GO HOME (POINTING AT DAN) AND WOULD CALL ME LATER! OH, THEN HE SAYS, I SNUCK OUT BEFORE I FINISHED THE ROOM! YOU BELIEVE THAT? WE WERE BOTH JUST SHAKING OUR HEADS IN DISBELIEF! WE BOTH SAY, "THAT SUCKS ASS DUDE!" WELL, HE IS GETTING OLDER, MAYBE HE'S GETTING ALTHEIMERS? I DON'T KNOW? WE NEVER TOLD JOE OR JACK ABOUT THIS! WELL, UNTIL NOW!! SORRY YOU GUYS BUT WE NEEDED A PLACE TO DRINK!!

HALLOWEEN

     HALLOWEEN WAS ALWAYS A BIG DAY FOR US! WE COULDN'T WAIT TO GET OUR HANDS ON ALL THAT FREE CANDY! WE WERE ALWAYS THINKING OF WAYS TO GET "MORE" THAN OUR SHARE! WE DIDN'T WANT TO STEAL OTHER KIDS BAGS! WE THOUGHT THAT WAS BULLSHIT WHEN WE HEARD ABOUT OLDER KIDS WAITING UNTIL THE END OF THE NIGHT AND THEN RUNNING BY AND SNATCHING SOME LITTLE KIDS BAG THAT THEY WORKED ALL NIGHT TO GET! EVEN WE WEREN'T THAT CRUEL! BUT WE HAD TO FIND A WAY TO GET MORE CANDY! ESPECIALLY THE HOUSES THAT GAVE OUT GOOD STUFF! WE ALREADY STARTED "TRICK OR TREATING" BEFORE IT WAS EVEN DARK TO GET A JUMP ON EVERYONE. BUT THAT STILL DIDN'T SEEM TO GET US THAT MUCH MORE. THEN WE HAD A GREAT IDEA. LET'S ALL TAKE 2 COSTUMES WITH US! IF WE FIND A HOUSE WITH GOOD CANDY, WE WILL WALK AROUND THE CORNER AND CHANGE COSTUMES! SINCE WE WERE "WHITE TRASH" SOME OF OUR COSTUMES WERE JUST A SHEET WITH EYE HOLES CUT OUT. YOU WERE A GHOST! AND YOU

CARRIED A PILLOW CASE TO CARRY YOUR CANDY IN, SO I GUESS YOU WERE A MATCHING SET! OTHERS WOULD JUST WEAR A OLD BASEBALL UNIFORM AND SAY THEY WERE A BASEBALL PLAYER. SOME WOULD JUST HAVE LIKE A 50 CENT PLASTIC MASK OF A DEVIL OR A CLOWN. ANYWAY, IF THEY HAD SOMETHING GOOD TO GIVE OUT, WE WOULD WALK AROUND THE CORNER AND SWITCH MASKS AROUND, MAYBE PUT ON A COWBOY HAT, SOMETHING. THESE COSTUMES MADE NO SENSE AT ALL! A "DEVIL COWBOY" OR AS A "BASEBALL GHOST?" STUPID! BUT WE WOULD GO BACK UP AND RING THE BELL. WE WOULD GET, OH MY, WHAT DO WE HAVE HERE? OR, DIDN'T WE SEE YOU ALL BEFORE? WE WOULD JUST PLAY DUMB (EASY FOR US) AND SAY NO, WE JUST STARTED! WE WOULD GET THE CANDY, BUT IT WAS GETTING HARDER AND HARDER! I THINK THE NEXT YEAR WE CARRIED A EXTRA PILLOW CASE AND WHEN WE GOT TO THE DOOR AND SAID TRICK OR TREAT, WE WOULD THEN SAY COULD WE GET A CANDY FOR MY LITTLE BROTHER WHIO IS SICK IN BED AND COULDN'T COME THIS YEAR? THAT WORKED BETTER! THEY FELT BAD AND SOMETIMES EVEN GAVE US TWO PIECES. SCORE!! ANYTHING TO GET MORE!!

DEAD MAN'S CURVE

I REMEMBER ONE SUMMER DAY THAT WAS ABOUT 104* AND HOT AS HELL. CODY AND DAN WERE THINKING OF WAYS TO "KEEP COOL" AND "PARTY" AT THE SAME TIME. THEY DECIDED TO GO "TUBING" DOWN THE RIVER! THEY INVITED ME BUT I HAD TO WORK! I HAD JUST CALLED IN SICK (TO GO DRINK) THE DAY BEFORE AND DIDN'T WANT TO PUSH IT! I WAS ON "THIN ICE" @ WORK AS IT WAS! ANYWAY, I WENT OFF TO WORK AND THOSE TWO TALKED ONE OF THE NEIGHBORS INTO NOT ONLY DRIVING THEM OUT OF TOWN AND UP THE HILL (SO THEY COULD FLOAT DOWN THE RIVER) BUT HE ALSO BOUGHT THEM THEIR BEER. THEY WERE "SHORT" BY ABOUT A BUCK BUT HE COVERED THIS AS WELL! MR. DINGLE WAS A COOL DUDE! HE WAS A RETIRED AIRCRAFT MECHANIC THAT REMEMBERED WHAT IT WAS LIKE BEING OUR AGE! CODY HAD PARKED HIS TRUCK AT THE BOTTOM OF THE RIVER BEFORE MR. DINGLE PICKED THEM UP SO THEY WOULD HAVE A WAY HOME

WHEN THEY WERE DONE. A LOT OF "WHITE TRASH" PEOPLE GOT INTO TUBING THAT SUMMER!

THEY UNLOADED THE TUBES, ICE CHEST AND WERE ON THEIR WAY! THE ICE CHEST FIT PERFECTLY IN THE "EXTRA" TUBE THEY BROUGHT AND MADE EASY ACCESS TO THE CHEAP ASS BEER THEY BOUGHT! THEY WERE HAVING A GOOD TIME JUST FLOATING DOWN THE RIVER AND "CATCHING A BUZZ." SOME OTHER "TUBERS" WERE BEHIND THEM BUT THEY NEVER LET THEM CATCH UP BECAUSE THEY DIDN'T WANT TO SHARE THEIR BEER WITH THEM! WHEN THEY WERE ALMOST AT THE END OF THEIR RIDE, THEY LOOKED OVER BY THE SIDE OF THE RIVER AND SAW SOMETHING FLOATING THERE. CODY SAID, "HEY DAN LOOK, IT'S A DEAD BODY!" THEY WERE ABOUT 30 FEET AWAY AND COULDN'T MAKE OUT WHAT IT WAS. THEY DECIDED IT WAS JUST A ROCK. THEY DIDN'T CARE, THEY WERE BUZZING PRETTY GOOD, THEY WERE SUNBURNED AND WERE HUNGRY! THEY KEPT GOING. ABOUT 5 MINUTES LATER, THE PEOPLE WHO WERE FLOATING BEHIND THEM STARTED YELLING WILDLY AND WERE TRYING TO GET THE GUYS ATTENTION. SINCE CODY AND DAN HAD JUST GOT OUT OF THE WATER THEY DECIDED TO WALK BACK ALONG THE WATER AND SEE WHAT THEY WANTED. THEY WERE OUT OF BEER SO NO WORRIES THERE. THE PEOPLE YELLING WERE ALL TOGETHER AT THE SPOT WHERE CODY SAID IT LOOKED LIKE A "DEAD BODY." THEY WALK UP AND DAN SAYS, "HOLY SHIT, IT IS A DEAD BODY!" LYING THEIR NAKED WAS A DEAD GUY WHO LOOKED LIKE HE HAD BEEN THEIR FOR AWHILE. HIS SKIN LOOKED LIKE YOUR HANDS LOOK WHEN YOU STAY IN THE WATER TOO LONG. THE SKIN WAS PALE WHITE. SOMEBODY NEEDED TO CALL THE COPS AND REPORT THIS! SINCE CODY AND DAN WERE DONE FLOATING THEY SAID THEY WOULD

GO FIND A PHONE AND CALL IT IN. REMEMBER, THERE WERE NO "CELL PHONES" BACK THEN. PAYPHONES TOOK DIMES! THEY THOUGHT THEY MIGHT BE ABLE TO GET INTO THE "APPEAL DEMOCRAT" FOR DISCOVERING A DEAD BODY. THEN THEY THOUGHT THEY MIGHT GET BUSTED FOR "UNDERAGE DRINKING" TOO! THEY DECIDED TO CALL THE SHERIFF'S OFFICE, REPORT IT AND HANG UP BEFORE THEY HAD TO GIVE THEIR NAMES! SO THEY CALLED IT IN AT A PAYPHONE IN TOWN (SO THEY COULDN'T TRACE THE CALL TO THEIR HOUSES) AND DROVE HOME BEFORE THEY GOT ASKED THEIR NAMES! IT WAS IN THE PAPER 2 DAYS LATER. THEY WERE ASKING FOR ANYBODY WITH INFORMATION ABOUT THE BODY TO COME TO THE SHERIFFS OFFICE AND TALK TO THEM. BULLSHIT! THAT WAS THE LAST TIME THEY WENT FLOATING DOWN THE RIVER THAT SUMMER!

WHERE ARE THEY NOW?

THE FOLLOWING IS AN UPDATE OF WHERE THE PEOPLE IN THIS BOOK ARE NOW, AS FAR AS WE KNOW!

MIKE: MIKE IS MARRIED TO HIS WONDERFUL WIFE "LISA." THEY HAVE BEEN MARRIED FOR 19 YEARS (TOGETHER FOR 23) AND HAVE TWO BEAUTIFUL CHILDREN, COLIN (18) AND AMANDA (12). MIKE IS ADDICTED TO "FACEBOOK" AND IS ON IT ALL THE TIME. IT SEEMS LIKE IT'S HIS "STAGE" WHERE HE CAN STILL BE A "COMEDIAN" WITHOUT LETTING HIS STAGE FRIGHT INTERFERE. MIKE LOST ONE OF HIS LEGS DUE TO COMPLICATIONS WITH DIABETES BUT DOESN'T LET THAT STOP HIM. HE PLANS TO DO SOME "INSPIRATIONAL SPEAKING" AND WOULD LOVE TO GET INTO "SUBSTANCE ABUSE" COUNSELING IN THE FUTURE. HE ENJOYS MOST SPORTS AND IS A DIEHARD 49ERS FAN! PROUD TO BE A VETERAN.

DAN: AFTER COLLEGE (CHICO STATE) DAN MOVED TO REDDING, WHERE HE MET HIS WIFE (LORI) OF 18 YEARS AND THEY HAVE 3 KIDS. DAN HAS SLOWED DOWN ON THE "PARTYING" AFTER GETTING IN AN "ALCOHOL RELATED ACCIDENT" IN COLLEGE. BUT WHO ARE WE KIDDING; DAN STILL LIKES TO HAVE A FEW BEERS! LIFE'S TOO SHORT! HE STILL ENJOYS SPORTS VERY MUCH. A DIEHARD DALLAS COWBOY FAN AND FANTASY FOOTBALL PLAYER. HIS LATEST PASSION IS COMPETING IN TRIATHLONS, THE "ULTIMATE RUSH IN LIFE!"

CODY LEWIS: CODY GOT MARRIED A FEW YEARS AFTER HIGHSCHOOL. HE WAS MARRIED FOR 20+ YEARS BEFORE RECENTLY GETTING DIVORCED. HE HAS A SON WHO IS NOW IN COLLEGE. CODY CHOSE TRUCK DRIVING AS A PROFESSION AND HAS WORKED FOR VARIOUS COMPANIES IN THE SACRAMENTO VALLEY. LOOKING FOR A CHANGE IN HIS LIFE, HE'S CONSIDERING GETTING INTO "LONG HAUL" TRUCKING AND MOVING OUT OF STATE. WE WISH CODY THE BEST OF LUCK IN THE FUTURE!

RONALD LOVE: AFTER HIGH SCHOOL, WE LOST TOUCH WITH RONALD UNTIL THE LAST FEW YEARS. DAN AND RONALD HAVE MET UP A FEW TIMES SINCE TO TALK FOOTBALL AND LAUGH ABOUT "THE OLD DAYS!" CURRENTLY LIVING IN IDAHO WITH HIS FAMILY, HE STILL ENJOYS HUNTING AND FISHING. THE SIZE OF THE FISH HE CATCHES GETS BIGGER EVERYTIME HE TELLS IT!

JACK JOHNSON: AFTER WORKING LOCALLY AS A MECHANIC FOR MANY YEARS, JACK FINALLY FULFILLED HIS DREAM OF MOVING TO ARKANSAS. HE CURRENTLY OWNS A RANCH IN FORT SMITH, WITH SEVERAL FARM ANIMALS. HE IS MARRIED AND THEY HAVE 3 BEAUTIFUL DAUGHTERS! JACK IS AN AVID MOTORCYCLE RIDER AND OWNS AN AWESOME HARLEY. AN AVID SPORTS FAN, HE STILL ROOTS FOR HIS "CALIFORNIA" TEAMS. HE CURRENTLY WORKS IN ELECTRONICS. JACK WAS BORN TO BE AN "OKIE!"

JOE JOHNSON: THE WORLD DOESN'T REALLY KNOW WHERE JOE IS OR WHAT HE DOES. HE'S BEEN MIA (MISSING IN ACTION) FOR SOME TIME. THERE ARE SOME "RANDOM" SPOTTINGS ON SOCIAL MEDIA (FACEBOOK) FROM TIME TO TIME, BUT VERY RARE. HE WAS DIAGNOSED WITH EXTREME ANXIETY A LONG

TIME AGO BUT WE ARE NOT SURE IF HE IS STILL DEALING WITH THIS OR NOT? ALWAYS AN AVID DODGER AND DALLAS COWBOY FAN, WE ASSUME HE IS STILL INTO SPORTS. JOE, IF YOU SOMEHOW READ THIS BOOK, PLEASE LET US KNOW HOW YOU ARE!

FINAL THOUGHTS

MIKE'S

I WANT TO THANK EVERYBODY WHO SUPPORTED US BY BUYING OUR BOOK! WE HAD A LOT OF FUN WRITING IT AND IT BROUGHT BACK SO MANY MEMORIES OF OUR CHILDHOOD. I WOULDN'T CHANGE IT A BIT. WE DIDN'T HAVE CELL PHONES OR COMPUTERS GROWING UP AND I'M GLAD WE DIDN'T. IT WAS A GREAT TIME WITHOUT THEM ! I'VE LEARNED ALOT OVER THE YEARS AND I VALUE MY FRIENDS I'VE MADE ALONG THE WAY. AS YOU CAN SEE BY READING THE BOOK, WE WERE SOME "BAD KIDS!" WE RAISED A LITTLE "HELL" BUT NOTHING TOO SEVERE. I WANT

YOU TO REMEMBER THAT IN TIME WE ALL GROW UP! SOMETIMES TAKING SOME OF US LONGER THAN OTHERS, BUT EVENTUALLY WE ALL DO. FAMILY IS EVERYTHING! YOU CAN'T TELL YOUR LOVED ONES THAT YOU LOVE THEM ENOUGH! YOU NEVER KNOW WHEN THE TIME MIGHT COME AND YOU WILL NO LONGER BE ABLE TO LET THEM KNOW!

LASTLY, I JUST WANT TO SAY THAT ALL THE THINGS THAT HAPPENED IN THIS BOOK WERE ABSOLUTELY TRUE! WE DIDN'T WANT TO "SUGARCOAT" THINGS TO GET LAUGHS, WE DIDN'T NEED TOO! IT STANDS ON ITS OWN!

DAN'S

      I HOPE THAT THE TITLE OF OUR BOOK DOESN'T "OFFEND" ANYONE. THE TERM "WHITE TRASH" HAS DIFFERENT MEANINGS TO DIFFERENT PEOPLE. TO ME, IT SIMPLY MEANS THAT WE WENT ABOUT THINGS

IN AN UNCONVENTIONAL MANNER. WE ALSO LIVED A CHILDHOOD WITH NO REGRETS!

MIKE AND I HAD THE GREATEST CHILDHOOD A KID COULD ASK FOR. IT DIDN'T MATTER THAT WE NEVER REALLY HAD MUCH MONEY. WE HAD OUR FRIENDS GROWING UP AND THAT WAS ENOUGH FOR US. MORE THAN ANYTHING, WE LAUGHED A LOT!! WE WOULD GO CRAZY IF WE HAD A DOLLAR, DON'T GET ME WRONG, BUT WE DIDN'T NEED IT!
MY REASONS FOR WANTING TO TELL OUR STORY ARE PLENTIFUL. I WANT PEOPLE TO REMEMBER THE GOOD OL' DAYS. A TIME WHEN IT WAS SAFE FOR KIDS TO BE OUT AFTER DARK. A TIME WHEN KIDS WERE ABLE TO PLAY OUTSIDE WITHOUT ANY FEAR OF WHAT WE KNOW TODAY.

I WANT GENERATIONS AND GENERATIONS TO REALIZE THAT THERE WAS A MOMENT IN TIME, PRIMARILY THE 70'S AND 80'S WHERE CHILDREN COULD HAVE FUN WITH VERY LITTLE RESOURCES. PLUS, I FEEL THE NEED TO TELL OUR STORY BEFORE MY MIND GOES ALL TO HELL! THE STORIES IN THIS BOOK TELL ONLY HALF OF IT ALL! I HOPE YOU ENJOY.

DEDICATIONS

MIKE'S

I WANT TO DEDICATE OUR 1ST BOOK TO SEVERAL PEOPLE. FIRST TO MY WIFE LISA AND TO MY 2 AWESOME KIDS, COLIN AND AMANDA, THE SUPPORT THEY GIVE ME ON A DAILY BASIS IS "PRICELESS!" TO MY MOM AND DAD WHO TAUGHT ME LOVE, COMPASSION, HONESTY AND PRIDE, AS WELL AS SO MANY OTHER THINGS. I CAN'T WAIT TO SEE THEM AGAIN IN HEAVEN SOMEDAY. MY (5) BROTHERS AND THEIR FAMILIES. THEY HAVE ALWAYS SUPPORTED MY "COMEDY" AND ENCOURAGED ME TO "ENTERTAIN" PEOPLE, EVERY CHANCE I GOT. THEY HAVE ALWAYS BEEN BEHIND ME 100%. THE MEN AND WOMEN OF THE ARMED FORCES, INCLUDING MY FELLOW VETERANS WHOM I SHARE A COMMON BOND WITH. THE BEST IN THE WORLD! LASTLY, TO ALL MY FRIENDS (TOO MANY TO NAME INDIVIDUALY) WHO I HAVE HAD THE PLEASURE OF STAYING IN CONTACT WITH, OR GETTING BACK IN CONTACT WITH THROUGH FACEBOOK AS WELL AS OTHER SOCIAL MEDIA OUTLETS. YOU MEAN THE WORLD TO ME!

DAN'S

I WOULD LIKE TO DEDICATE THIS BOOK TO EVERYONE WHO HAS HELPED SHAPE MY LIFE INTO WHAT IT IS TODAY; FROM MY PARENTS TO MY BROTHERS, TO MY FRIENDS AND CLASSMATES, AND TO THOSE GREAT TEACHERS THAT I HAD ALONG THE WAY. YOU KNOW WHO YOU ARE. I CAN'T FORGET

ABOUT MY COACHES. THANK YOU! THANK GOD FOR SPORTS, FOR WITHOUT THEM I MAY HAVE DRANK MYSELF TO DEATH. FINALLY TO MY WONDERFUL WIFE LORI, AND TO MY THREE AMAZING KIDS, LINDSEY, RYAN AND KAYLYNN, AS WELL AS TO MY 2 INCREDIBLE GRANDKIDS, LINCOLN AND MACI, I AM VERY THANKFUL.